Live Luxe!

Living Luxe

GLUTEN FREE

Living Luxe

GLUTEN FREE

SALUT
STUDIO

·MICHELLE LEE·

Published by Salut Studio LLC
www.salutstudio.com

10 9 8 7 6 5 4 3 2 1

Library of Congress Control Number: 2014953820

ISBN 978-0-9908817-0-4
Ebook ISBN 978-0-9908817-1-1

Written by Michelle Lee

Photographs on pages 1, 3, 4, 5, 6, 71, 111, 192, 214, 228, 243, 244 and back cover (photograph of Michelle) by Marianne Wilson Photography
All other photographs by Michelle Lee

Cover design by Kat Tushim

Ciao font used for recipe names, section headings, tip headings, and dedication designed by Juan A. Zamarripa

Printed in Canada

The check-tree logo is your assurance that the paper in this document meets the rigorous environmental and social standards of the Forest Stewardship Council (FSC).

TO STEVE, MY HUSBAND, BEST FRIEND, AND PARTNER IN (FOOD) CRIME

MENU

SALADS & SIDES 119

PRELUDE

The recipes in this book were inspired by my husband, Steve, who developed sensitivities to gluten and lactose as well as some nuts and seeds several years into our marriage. As a couple, one of our shared pastimes has always been eating – everything from college-town bar foods to trademark dishes in Europe's oldest restaurants to exotic plates in remote Asian fishing villages. And we grew adept at replicating many of those flavors at home. So when we learned about Steve's food sensitivities, we were concerned we'd no longer be able to enjoy something we'd always loved, great – even luxurious – food.

We eventually realized that a gluten-free and lactose-free diet didn't mean we had to give up eating what we loved. Yes, we had to alter our diet a bit, but that alteration presented opportunities to reinvent some old recipes, step outside of our comfort zones, and explore even more culinary terrain.

We now eat tastier, healthier meals than we did before. We both feel better than ever. And it's hard to imagine we haven't always eaten this way!

This cookbook shares recipes I've developed on the food journey Steve and I have taken since the time his diet had to change. It's intended to provide you with a leg up on creating fantastic, healthy meals that celebrate the richness of ingredients that don't contain gluten or lactose.

These recipes are not only designed for nutritious diets, they're also engineered for discerning palates. They're perfect for people Living Luxe Gluten Free. No hassle, no compromise, just great food.

I hope you enjoy the dishes in this book, and I hope they inspire you to try exciting new recipes without gluten or lactose.

Eat well. Feel great. Live luxe!

LIVING LUXE GLUTEN FREE

While this cookbook is designed to accommodate gluten and lactose sensitivities, my recipes are also ideal for anyone interested in improving the nutritional quality – and tastiness – of their diet.

Most dishes are based upon natural, healthy ingredients like vegetables, fruits, fish, and ancient grains. What you won't find are recipes calling for lots of processed foods, preservatives, sugars, trans fats, or sodium. Even foods I've created to satisfy cravings for fare like fritters and Buffalo wings have been engineered with a healthy diet in mind.

My recipes align in some respects with a Mediterranean diet, and many can be part of Paleo-compliant, vegetarian, vegan, or low-sodium eating regimens. To make this cookbook user-friendly, I've indicated for each recipe whether it's Paleo, vegetarian, vegan, or low-sodium using the following icons:

P Paleo   **VE** Vegan

S Low Sodium   **VG** Vegetarian

My approach to cooking and ingredient selection reflects in part my time living in Spain and in part my own observations about how my husband and I feel when we do (or don't) eat certain foods. I'm happiest when I have plenty of energy for my workouts and for the surprises that seem to crop up each day, as well as when I can think clearly at work and at home. My recipes provide long-lasting energy and no drag, without sacrificing flavor.

I've prioritized straightforward preparation in creating my recipes. They're perfect for anyone who wants to eat gourmet foods without the time and energy of gourmet prep. I spent the first decade of my career as a business consultant, which meant my working hours were long, unpredictable, and often bled into the weekend – I know what it's like to not feel like making dinner!

It should be noted that my recipes do not call for gluten- or lactose-heavy ingredients. However, certain ingredients may contain low levels of gluten or lactose due to the way they're handled as part of our food supply. Additionally, low-lactose cheeses that tend to be well-tolerated by those with lactose sensitivities may be called for in some recipes. Such ingredients and the recipes in which they're found may not be appropriate for everyone. Each person's particular diet sensitivities and needs should be taken into account before preparing or serving any recipe in this book.

KEY INGREDIENTS

As I've learned through my many years, trials, and failures in the kitchen, ingredient quality can have a significant – even overwhelming – impact on a finished dish. For certain ingredients like fish or meats, the input/output relationship is obvious. Even for apparently "minor" ingredients, though, I've found quality can count for a lot.

But quality can be difficult to find, high-quality products can be expensive, and products of dubious character can be enveloped in slick and misleading marketing. To ease ingredient selection, I've included a listing of my "Favorite Products" that can help make dishes great.

Aside from my favorite products, here's what I look for when shopping:

- For animal-based foods, I try to purchase wild-caught fish, grassfed beef, free-range chicken, and eggs from hens fed a diet supportive of omega-3 fatty acid production.

- For fruits and vegetables, I seek out organic produce, with emphasis on produce whose quality is most impacted by organic cultivation. Potatoes and carrots, for instance, can leech soil toxins, so I prioritize organic purchases of these. I also go organic with produce whose edible portions are not protected by outer skins that go uneaten.

- When I purchase packaged goods, I stay away from those laden with preservatives, sodium, sugar, artificial flavors, or coloring agents. Since this sometimes diminishes shelf life, I recommend freezing foods like loaves of bread not likely to be entirely consumed in the first couple of days after purchase.

FAVORITE PRODUCTS

My household's transition to a gluten-free and lactose-free diet has meant lots of product testing. Below is a list of products that have aced my exams. I recommend these ingredients because they taste great, have familiar cooking characteristics, and help cut down on effort in the kitchen – all while offering the health benefits of gluten-free and lactose-free eating!

- Annie Chun's Gluten Free Teriyaki Sauce: With this gluten-free alternative to traditional teriyaki sauce, you give up the gluten but keep every bit of flavor.

- Belfiore Cheese Russian Style Farmers Cheese: I was skeptical when I learned that farmers cheese is well tolerated by lactose-sensitive individuals, but my husband eats this cheese with no problem. It's great for desserts and as a substitute for feta cheese or even cream cheese. And it's all-natural.

- Canyon Bakehouse Gluten Free Burger Buns: Though not exactly a health food, these slightly buttery, delicious burger buns hit the spot when a "regular-tasting" gluten-free burger bun is in order.

- Daiya Cheddar Style Shreds: Very good cheddar flavor, vegan, and conveniently pre-grated, this product is my go-to when cheddar taste is necessary and lactose levels must be kept at zero.

- Daiya Deliciously Dairy Free Plain Cream Cheese Style Spread: It's safe for lactose-free and vegan diets, and it's so versatile that it tastes great in recipes ranging from spinach and artichoke dip to cream cheese frosting.

- Daiya Swiss Style Slices: This is my choice for Swiss cheese flavor in lactose-free form.

- Dorot Frozen Crushed Garlic cubes: These freezer-section cubes eliminate the job of peeling fresh garlic cloves and have a much better shelf life than fresh garlic. The cubes can be used almost any time minced or crushed garlic is called for; each cube is equal to one clove. Say goodbye to fingers that smell like garlic after cooking!

- Earth Balance Natural Buttery Spread: It tastes just like butter, but it's vegan, gluten-free, and non-dairy. Whenever I need lactose-free butter, I reach for this.

- Enjoy Life Semi-Sweet Chocolate Mega Chunks: I think these might be safe for nearly every food allergy, and the best part is that they taste just as good as other top-of-the-line chocolate chips.

- Follow Your Heart Vegan Gourmet Monterey Jack: This non-dairy cheese substitute melts just like the real thing, tastes fantastic, and can be easily grated. This is the product I reach for whenever I'm looking for Monterey Jack flavor.

- Glutino Original Bagel Chips: When crushed, they make perfect breadcrumbs that taste great.

- Green Valley Organics Lactose Free Sour Cream: This sour cream contains no soy or gluten. It's all-natural sour cream prepared with lactase enzyme.

- Just Mayo and Trader Joe's Organic Mayonnaise: Both of these have a round, mild taste that works perfectly in aioli recipes. Just Mayo is a delicious option for vegan dishes.

- Kite Hill Cassucio Soft Fresh Nut Milk Cheese: When zero lactose is required but feta-like cheese texture is also necessary, I reach for this product.

- Lactaid: I love the simplicity of the Lactaid formula. It's my go-to milk substitute.

- Organic Valley Lactose Free Half and Half: This product is great for cooking because it imparts a nice and even richness to foods.

- Pamela's Classic Vanilla Cake Mix: The Pamela's brand lineup of baking products is high quality, and the vanilla cake mix may be my favorite product of the bunch. I use this cake mix for great texture and flavor.

- Trader Joe's Baker Josef's Organic Coconut Flour: For those on gluten-free diets, excessive exposure to arsenic from rice-based products may be a concern. This flour is a great alternative to gluten-free all-purpose flour made from rice, and I often use it in fried dishes as a gluten-free all-purpose flour.

- Trader Joe's Chili Pepper Sauce: This sauce is an excellent, lower-sodium alternative to Frank's RedHot Original Cayenne Pepper Sauce (which I also recommend for its great Buffalo-style flavor).

- Trader Joe's Organics Organic Heirloom Tomatoes: From a flavor perspective, tomatoes don't get any better than this. They're worth every penny.

- Trader Joe's Rolled Oats: They're whole grain, gluten-free, wheat-free, and dairy-free. What's not to love about that?

- Trader Joe's Sweet Chili Sauce: A fantastic way to add Asian flavor to a variety of dishes.

- Udi's Gluten Free Bread: Of all the gluten-free breads I've tasted, Udi's is the hands-down winner for having a consistency that's soft and fluffy like normal bread. It also relies less on brown rice flour than some other brands.

- Udi's Thin & Crispy Pizza Crusts: Udi's pizza crusts have great flavor and a consistency just like regular pizza crust. I love how the edges become perfectly crisped when baked in the oven.

- Van's Multigrain Crispy Whole Grain Baked Crackers: When you're in the mood for crackers, these taste just like regular crackers but they're gluten-free, dairy-free, and contain no artificial colors or flavors.

- WayFare We Can't Say It's Sour Cream: A tasty, vegan alternative to Green Valley Organics Lactose Free Sour Cream, this product works very well in dips, such as spinach and artichoke dip and onion dip.

Doesn't it often seem like appetizers are even more delicious than the main courses for which they're meant to build anticipation? I can't tell you how many times I've taken the first bite of an entrée only to wish I could go back for seconds of the starter!

I hope these recipes help explain my obsession with appetizers, and I hope you'll find that some of these dishes' flavors and textures are interesting enough that they become a regular part of your cooking.

Of course, I also hope you'll manage to move on to an entrée after you've finished the starter dish...though I couldn't blame you if not.

BUFFALO SPROUTS

Buffalo wings have been a long-time favorite in my household. Unfortunately, wings are often floured, and even when they're not, they usually serve up as much saturated fat and cholesterol as they do heat. This recipe banishes the bad stuff but keeps the spice. Easy to put together, my Buffalo hummus sauce transforms Brussels sprouts into something irresistible. The only downside to this dish is that the entire batch often disappears in one sitting.

1 Preheat oven to 450 degrees. Line a baking sheet with foil.

2 Place sprouts on baking sheet, drizzle with olive oil, and toss to coat. Sprinkle with salt and pepper and toss. Arrange in a single layer on baking sheet, cut side down.

3 Bake sprouts for 15 to 20 minutes, stirring halfway through baking time. Don't worry about keeping them all cut side down. Sprouts are ready when browned on edges.

4 Mix together Buffalo dip ingredients in a small bowl. Serve immediately or cover and refrigerate until ready to serve.

SPROUTS

1 lb. whole Brussels sprouts, stems removed, cut in half lengthwise
2 tbsp. extra virgin olive oil
¼ tsp. salt
¼ tsp. lemon pepper seasoning or ground black pepper

BUFFALO DIP

10 oz. red pepper hummus dip
6+ tbsp. hot sauce
4 tsp. lactose-free butter, room temperature
1 tsp. white balsamic vinegar
¼ to ½ tsp. cayenne pepper
¼ to ½ tsp. garlic powder

TIP

I recommend using Trader Joe's Smooth and Creamy Roasted Red Pepper Hummus for this recipe.

Calories: 190; Total Fat (g): 13; Saturated Fat (g): 1; Cholesterol (mg): 0; Sodium (mg): 900; Potassium (mg): 240; Total Carbohydrate (g): 16; Fiber (g): 5; Sugar (g): 3; Protein (g): 5. Content per serving. Assumes 6 servings.

SERVES 4 to 6
PAIRING Omission Lager
EFFORT Easy enough to make on a work night
ACTIVE PREP 10 to 15 minutes

CHORIZO QUESO FUNDIDO

A Mexican restaurant in Sedona is so popular that a line to get in often wraps around the building – before the place even opens. One big attraction is their queso fundido, which I've never stopped thinking about. My recipe pays lactose-free homage to their cheesy, sausage-y masterpiece. This dip is filled with chunks of chorizo, bell pepper, and onion... perfect with corn chips or tortillas. It's filling enough to be a meal, and you don't even have to wait in line to get it!

1 tsp. canola oil

1 6-inch chorizo link, chopped into ¼-inch chunks

1 green bell pepper, thinly sliced

1 small yellow onion, thinly sliced

5 oz. lactose-free Monterey Jack, sliced into thin squares

Smoked paprika

SERVES 4
EFFORT Mid-level, and worth it
ACTIVE PREP 15 to 20 minutes
PAIRING See my Marvaritas recipe

1 Move oven rack to top and preheat oven to 425 degrees.

2 Heat a small cast-iron skillet on stovetop over medium-high heat and add canola oil. When oil is heated, add chorizo and sauté until just browned on the outside, about 5 minutes. Using a slotted spoon, remove chorizo and set aside on a plate. Add green pepper and onion to skillet, and sauté in juices of chorizo until onion is translucent, about 5 to 7 minutes.

3 Remove skillet from heat and place onions and pepper on plate with chorizo. Place a small layer of Monterey Jack in the bottom of skillet and top with about a third of the chorizo, pepper, and onion mix. Add another layer of Monterey Jack, then chorizo mix, and repeat process until all ingredients are in skillet. Sprinkle to taste with paprika.

4 Place skillet in oven and bake until Monterey Jack is melted and beginning to bubble and turn brown, about 10 to 15 minutes. Remove from oven and serve in skillet, leaving oven mitt on handle for safety. Scoop dip onto tortilla chips or soft corn tortillas.

TIP
I recommend using Follow Your Heart Vegan Gourmet Monterey Jack for this recipe.

Calories: 180; Total Fat (g): 15; Saturated Fat (g): 2; Cholesterol (mg): 14; Sodium (mg): 320; Potassium (mg): 110; Total Carbohydrate (g): 8; Fiber (g): 4; Sugar (g): 3; Protein (g): 6. Content per serving. Assumes 4 servings.

PATATAS BRAVAS

Jet-lagged during my first night in Madrid, all I wanted was to go to bed. But I was determined to try some tapas before falling asleep. I dragged myself to a bar near the Las Ventas bullring and ordered patatas bravas. Sleepy no more! Crispy and chewy, spicy and savory, and topped with a comforting garlic mayonnaise, they were gone in an instant. I had to make the dish at home. Though traditionally fried in chili oil, my recipe captures the same Spanish flavors without frying or jet lag.

1 Preheat oven to 425 degrees.

2 Place potatoes in 8-by-8-inch glass baking dish. Drizzle with olive oil and toss to coat. Sprinkle with pimenton dulce, pepper, salt, cayenne pepper, and chili powder and toss. Bake for 30 minutes, stirring halfway through cooking time. Potatoes are ready when wedges' centers are soft when poked with a fork.

3 In a small bowl, whisk together garlic mayonnaise ingredients.

4 When potatoes are cooked through, remove from oven and place in a small serving bowl. Drizzle desired amounts of hot sauce and garlic mayonnaise on potatoes. Serve immediately with remaining garlic mayonnaise as dipping sauce.

PATATAS BRAVAS
8 to 10 new potatoes, cut into ¾-inch wedges
½ to 1 tbsp. extra virgin olive oil
¼ tsp. pimenton dulce (i.e., sweet smoked paprika)
¼ tsp. ground black pepper
¼ tsp. salt
Cayenne pepper, to taste
Chili powder, to taste
Hot sauce

GARLIC MAYONNAISE
¼ cup mayonnaise
1 garlic clove, crushed
Juice from ¼ lemon
Dash of salt

TIP
For tapas-style snacking, serve on a platter with a toothpick in each potato wedge. Use Just Mayo for vegan prep.

Calories: 210; Total Fat (g): 10; Saturated Fat (g): 1; Cholesterol (mg): 7; Sodium (mg): 180; Potassium (mg): 730; Total Carbohydrate (g): 27; Fiber (g): 3; Sugar (g): 1; Protein (g): 3. Content per serving. Assumes 6 servings.

SERVES 4 to 6
EFFORT Easy enough for a busy (or jet lagged) night
ACTIVE PREP 5 to 10 minutes
PAIRING Daura Damm

SPINACHOKE DIP

Spinach and artichoke dip once was a favorite during college football season. However, since it usually contains lactose and is served with bread, my husband's food sensitivities rendered the creamy delight off-limits. This recipe restores spinach and artichoke dip's place on Saturday afternoons. Free of lactose and gluten, Spinachoke Dip is great whenever the gridiron's on TV. The dip has reached perfection when the edges are brown and the consistency is thick enough to cling to a tortilla chip.

1¼ cups lactose-free Monterey Jack, grated

6 oz. spinach leaves, stems removed and leaves roughly chopped

9 oz. canned artichoke hearts, drained and chopped

⅔ cup lactose-free cream cheese at room temperature

½ cup lactose-free sour cream

¼ cup mayonnaise

4 tsp. garlic, minced (about 4 large cloves)

Smoked paprika

1 Preheat oven to 375 degrees.

2 In a large bowl, mix Monterey Jack, spinach, and artichoke hearts. Set aside. In a separate bowl, mix cream cheese, sour cream, mayonnaise, and garlic. Combine both bowls' contents and stir mixture together.

3 Pour mixture into a lightly greased 8-by-8-inch glass baking dish. Press with a spoon to spread evenly. Sprinkle with smoked paprika to taste.

4 Bake until spinach has wilted and cheeses are melted and browning around edges of dish, about 35 to 40 minutes. Serve with tortilla chips for dipping.

SERVES 6 to 8
EFFORT Easy enough to throw together right before guests arrive
ACTIVE PREP 10 to 15 minutes
PAIRING Pinot Grigio

TIP

For vegan prep, use Just Mayo, Follow Your Heart Vegan Gourmet Monetery Jack, and vegan cream cheese and sour cream.

Calories: 300; Total Fat (g): 27; Saturated Fat (g): 12; Cholesterol (mg): 23; Sodium (mg): 450; Potassium (mg): 140; Total Carbohydrate (g): 9; Fiber (g): 2; Sugar (g): 1; Protein (g): 4. Content per serving. Assumes 8 servings.

MARROWBONES AND GARLIC TOAST

At a bar in downtown Los Angeles, my husband and I encountered roasted marrowbones on the menu. Having never eaten them before, we were equal parts intrigued and uncertain. But one round of drinks later, our adventurous sides had gotten the best of us. And what a treat! Like the juiciest and most flavorful bite of steak, the marrow melted in our mouths. This recipe makes the experience an easy one to replicate at home, but beware: these marrowbones are addictive!

1 Preheat oven to 450 degrees. Line a baking sheet with foil and place marrowbones on top of foil, cut side up.

2 Bake marrowbones until marrow is soft, about 20 to 25 minutes. Marrow will look fatty and soft and be easily scooped out of the bones with a spoon or knife when properly cooked.

3 Combine parsley and onion in a small serving bowl. Whisk together olive oil and lemon, then pour over the parsley and onion mixture and stir.

4 Mix butter with garlic and spread garlic butter on toasted bread quarters.

5 When marrowbones are ready, remove from oven, sprinkle tops with sea salt, and serve immediately. Be careful when removing bones from baking sheet, as they will be extremely hot.

6 To eat, scoop marrow out of bones with spoon or knife and top with parsley salad. Spread on garlic toast as desired.

4 to 6 3-inch long beef marrow-bone rounds

½ cup parsley, chopped

2 tbsp. red onion, diced

2 tbsp. extra virgin olive oil

2 tsp. fresh-squeezed lemon juice

2 tbsp. lactose-free butter, room temperature

1 garlic clove, minced

2 to 3 slices gluten-free bread, toasted and sliced into quarters

Sea salt

SERVES 4 to 6
EFFORT Can be done a weeknight
ACTIVE PREP 15 to 20 minutes
PAIRING Omission Pale Ale

TIP

Given their nutritional heft, I like to serve marrowbones as part of a lighter, tapas-style meal. Omit garlic toast for Paleo prep.

Calories: 510; Total Fat (g): 52; Saturated Fat (g): 1; Cholesterol (mg): 0; Sodium (mg): 30; Potassium (mg): 30; Total Carbohydrate (g): 7; Fiber (g): 1; Sugar (g): 1; Protein (g): 1. Content per serving. Assumes 6 servings.

BERENJENAS CON MIELE

Have you ever been in love with something and just not known it yet? It turns out that was the case for me with fried eggplant: love at first bite. Served in pieces *pequeñas* with honey drizzled on top, berenjenas con miele always seems to stir up passion. Who knew eggplant and honey would be such a fantastic combination? Well, I didn't, but now you do...prepare to be swept off your feet.

1 eggplant, sliced into 1-square inch pieces ¼-inch thick
Salt
½ cup gluten-free all-purpose flour
½ cup gluten-free breadcrumbs
½ liter extra virgin olive oil
3 eggs, beaten in a wide, shallow bowl
Honey

SERVES 4 to 6
EFFORT Don't try this on a week-night! Eggplant drains for 2 hours.
ACTIVE PREP 35 to 45 minutes
PAIRING See my Tinto de Sangria recipe

TIP
To keep eggplant warm, place in oven on low heat, about 250 degrees, until ready to serve.

1 Place a colander atop a rimmed baking sheet. Layer eggplant slices in colander, sprinkling salt on each slice. Place heavy saucers or dishes on top of eggplant slices and let sit for 2 hours. Then wipe salt and surface moisture from eggplant and lay pieces out on paper towel.

2 Combine flour and breadcrumbs plus a little salt (¼ tsp. or less) in a shallow bowl and mix thoroughly. Set beside stovetop.

3 Heat a large, deep skillet over medium heat and pour olive oil in skillet (should be approximately ½-inch deep). When oil is shimmering, dredge eggplant in flour mixture and then in egg. Slide coated eggplant into hot oil. Cook until outsides are golden brown, about 3 to 5 minutes per eggplant slice, turning once with tongs. Once browned, place eggplant pieces on paper towel to absorb excess oil. Work in batches.

4 When all slices have been cooked, place eggplant in serving dish and drizzle with honey. Serve immediately.

Calories: 180; Total Fat (g): 7; Saturated Fat (g): 1; Cholesterol (mg): 108; Sodium (mg): 220; Potassium (mg): 130; Total Carbohydrate (g): 24; Fiber (g): 3; Sugar (g): 5; Protein (g): 5. Content per serving. Assumes 6 servings.

GLORIOUS GUACAMOLE

With its etymological roots in the language of the Aztecs, it's difficult not to imagine Aztec warriors fueling up on this nutritious dish before battle. Plenty of healthy fats, anti-oxidants, and anti-inflamatory properties make guacamole a warrior itself. But it has a civil side as well. The creaminess, flourish of jalapeno and garlic, and sweetness of lime guarantee a welcoming salvo of flavors. My Marvaritas are a natural auxiliary for this dip, whether you're building an empire or hosting a party.

2 ripe avocadoes, diced

¼ cup ripe tomato, diced

3 garlic cloves, minced

1 tbsp. salsa

Juice from ½ lime

¼ tsp. cumin

¼ tsp. salt

¼ to ½ jalapeño pepper, diced (optional)

2 tsp. cilantro, chopped

1 Place avocadoes in a large, deep bowl and mash with a fork.

2 Stir in tomato, garlic, salsa, lime juice, cumin, salt, and jalapeño pepper (if using). Continue mashing and stirring until a smooth dip is created (a few small chunks of avocado are okay).

3 Stir in cilantro and serve immediately with tortilla chips, atop tacos, or alongside any Latin dish.

SERVES 4

EFFORT This dish can be whipped up any time

ACTIVE PREP 10 to 15 minutes

PAIRING See any of my margarita recipes – you can't go wrong

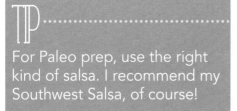

For Paleo prep, use the right kind of salsa. I recommend my Southwest Salsa, of course!

Calories: 170; Total Fat (g): 15; Saturated Fat (g): 2; Cholesterol (mg): 0; Sodium (mg): 170; Potassium (mg): 510; Total Carbohydrate (g): 11; Fiber (g): 7; Sugar (g): 1; Protein (g): 2. Content per serving. Assumes 4 servings.

BONUS TIP

When covered and stored in the refrigerator, guacamole dip turns brown. To solve this issue, place the dip in a resealable container, pressing into bottom of container to remove any air bubbles. I like to place a layer of plastic wrap on top of dip and push air out with fingers or a spoon. Once the air has been pressed out, gently pour a half-inch of lukewarm water on top of the dip, cover, and store in the refrigerator anywhere from a few hours to overnight. When you're ready to eat, pour out the water, stir, and serve.

ROASTED GARLIC AND FLATBREAD

After a day of hiking in the Arizona desert, I lugged myself to a restaurant in town and ordered the first thing I saw on the menu. Roasted garlic accompanied by baked Brie and berries – and the unlikely pairing did not disappoint. For this recipe, I've substituted lactose-free Monterey Jack for Brie and used gluten-free pizza crust for flatbread. This appetizer is so good you might be willing to trek across the desert to get it – but now you won't have to!

2 garlic heads, top ¼ inch of cloves chopped off with outer skin removed

1 tsp. extra virgin olive oil for garlic + 1 tsp. for pizza

1 10-inch gluten-free pizza crust, such as Udi's Thin & Crispy Pizza Crust

Pinch of dried rosemary

5 oz. lactose-free Monterey Jack, sliced into ¼-inch thick wedges

2 cups mixed strawberries, blueberries, and raspberries

1 Preheat oven to 400 degrees.

2 Place each garlic head on a separate sheet of foil and drizzle ½ tsp. olive oil on cut end of each head. Rub olive oil over the cloves to ensure it coats the tops.

3 Wrap foil entirely around each garlic head and place on a baking sheet. Bake until cloves are soft, about 30 to 35 minutes. Cloves are ready when they can be removed from their skin with a butter knife and spread easily as a topping on bread.

4 When garlic is ready, remove from oven and leave wrapped in foil. Reduce oven temperature to 375.

5 Drizzle 1 tsp. olive oil over pizza crust and lightly sprinkle with a pinch of dried rosemary. Top evenly with slices of Monterey Jack.

6 Bake pizza until crust is just heated through and cheese has started to melt, about 5 to 7 minutes. Remove from oven and slice like a pie. Serve immediately with garlic as a spread and berries for topping.

SERVES 4 to 6
EFFORT Easy
ACTIVE PREP 5 to 10 minutes
PAIRING Gloria Ferrar Brut

TIP

For vegan prep, use Follow Your Heart Vegan Gourmet Monterey Jack. For low-lactose prep, use Manchego Añejo.

Calories: 180; Total Fat (g): 9; Saturated Fat (g): 0; Cholesterol (mg): 0; Sodium (mg): 240; Potassium (mg): 70; Total Carbohydrate (g): 22; Fiber (g): 3; Sugar (g): 6; Protein (g): 3. Content per serving. Assumes 6 servings.

HOMEMADE BBQ CHIPS AND ONION DIP

According to my husband's hierarchy of chips, any chip is good, BBQ chips are preferable, and homemade BBQ chips rest atop the chip pyramid. So when I introduced him to homemade BBQ chips and onion dip, the combo blew his mind. This snack is infinitely crave-able, so it's a great appetizer for summer get-togethers with friends and family, who, from time to time, could stand to have their minds blown! I like these chips best when they're warm, so serve 'em while they're hot.

POTATO CHIPS
2 tsp. brown sugar
1 tsp. smoked paprika
¼ tsp. salt
¼ tsp. onion powder
2 baking potatoes, sliced into thin rounds
2 tbsp. canola oil

ONION DIP
¼ cup lactose-free sour cream
½ yellow onion, diced and sautéed
2 to 3 scallions, finely chopped
1 garlic clove, crushed
1 tbsp. mayonnaise
½ tsp. ground black pepper
¼ tsp. or less salt

1 In a small bowl, mix together brown sugar, paprika, salt, and onion powder. Pour spices into a large re-sealable bag and set aside.

2 Mix onion dip ingredients in a small bowl. Cover and refrigerate until ready to serve.

3 Place sliced potatoes in a large mixing bowl. Drizzle oil over potatoes and toss to coat thoroughly.

4 Lightly coat a microwave-safe plate with oil. Working in batches, place potato slices in a single layer on plate and microwave on high for 3 minutes. Flip potatoes and continue cooking in microwave on high for about 2 more minutes or until centers of potatoes begin to brown. Place potatoes on a paper-towel lined plate to cool.

5 Place slightly-cooled potato slices in spice bag and shake to coat with seasoning. Serve immediately.

SERVES 4 to 6
EFFORT Probably better to save for the weekend
ACTIVE PREP 30 to 35 minutes
PAIRING Lemonade or see my Electric Strawberry Lemonade recipe

Chips: Calories: 150; Total Fat (g): 7; Saturated Fat (g): 1; Cholesterol (mg): 0; Sodium (mg): 80; Potassium (mg): 530; Total Carbohydrate (g): 21; Fiber (g): 2; Sugar (g): 2; Protein (g): 2. Content per serving. Assumes 6 servings.

Dip: Calories: 60; Total Fat (g): 5; Saturated Fat (g): 3; Cholesterol (mg): 13; Sodium (mg): 100; Potassium (mg): 40; Total Carbohydrate (g): 2; Fiber (g): 0; Sugar (g): 1; Protein (g): 1. Content per serving. Assumes 6 servings.

To prevent raw potatoes from browning during preparation, slice each batch of potatoes just before cooking in microwave.

For vegan prep, use Just Mayo and vegan sour cream.

PAN CON TOMATE

A popular standby at Spanish restaurants is pan con tomate (bread with tomato). Typically accompanied by orange juice and coffee at breakfast or a small beer and entree at lunchtime, pan con tomate is deceptively simple. Yes, it's just tomato puree spread onto toast, but the recipe can go awry if the ingredients aren't fresh and carefully selected. Heirloom tomatoes are key to making this dish a success.

2 tbsp. extra virgin olive oil

1 garlic clove, minced

2 to 3 heirloom tomatoes, peeled and quartered (see "Encore" section for peeling instructions)

2 tbsp. lactose-free butter

1 tsp. granulated sugar

Salt

Ground black pepper

4 to 6 slices gluten-free bread or baguette, sliced

1 Heat olive oil in a large, non-stick skillet over medium to medium-high heat. Add garlic and stir, cooking for about 30 seconds. Add tomatoes, butter, and sugar. Add salt and pepper to taste. Continue to cook until tomatoes are heated through, about 10 to 15 minutes.

2 Place tomato mixture in food processor and process until mixture is fairly smooth (a few tomato chunks are okay).

3 When ready to serve, toast bread to liking. Top with desired amount of tomate and drizzle with olive oil. Tomate may be covered and stored in refrigerator for up to 2 days.

SERVES 4 to 6
EFFORT Easy enough to make on a weeknight and eat the next morning for breakfast
ACTIVE PREP 20 to 25 minutes
PAIRING Fresh orange juice in the morning; Daura Damm in the afternoon

Tomate tastes best when served at room temperature. For vegan prep, use Earth Balance Natural Buttery Spread.

Calories: 200; Total Fat (g): 10; Saturated Fat (g): 2; Cholesterol (mg): 0; Sodium (mg): 120; Potassium (mg): 150; Total Carbohydrate (g): 23; Fiber (g): 2; Sugar (g): 5; Protein (g): 3. Content per serving. Assumes 6 servings.

TIP

Gluten-free dipping sauce, like Trader Joe's Sweet Chili Sauce or Trader Joe's Mango Chutney, works well in place of hot sauce. Barbecue sauce is also a great option.

NO BONES ABOUT 'EM BUFFALO TENDERS

Gluten-free Buffalo wings can be hard to come by, and tasty ones can be exceptionally rare. After taste-testing dozens of gluten-free wings, I've determined most options should be permanently grounded. So I developed my own recipe for that perfect Buffalo flavor, without the worry of gluten or lactose. While these tenders may not be wings, they're juicy and flavorful enough to help snacking really take flight. I like to make these tenders as accompaniment to NBA playoffs and pizza.

1 Preheat oven to 250 degrees.

2 Mix sauce ingredients in a small bowl and set aside.

3 Mix flour, breadcrumbs, pepper, salt, and paprika in a wide, shallow bowl and set aside.

4 In a large, deep skillet, heat oil over medium-high heat until it begins to shimmer. Working in batches, first dredge chicken in egg and then in flour mixture. Place coated chicken in skillet and cook until outsides are golden brown and meat is cooked through, about 5 minutes per side (use tongs when flipping tenders).

5 Place cooked chicken pieces on a plate lined with paper towels to drain. Once drained, arrange tenders in an oven-safe dish and place in oven to keep warm.

6 Pour sauce over tenders and toss to coat. Enjoy immediately.

SAUCE

6+ tbsp. hot sauce

4 tsp. lactose-free butter, room temperature

1 tsp. white balsamic vinegar

Cayenne pepper (to taste)

Garlic powder (to taste)

TENDERS

½ cup gluten-free all-purpose flour

½ cup gluten-free breadcrumbs

1 tsp. ground black pepper

½ tsp. salt

½ tsp. smoked paprika

1 cup canola oil

1 lb. boneless, skinless chicken breast tenders

1 egg, lightly beaten in a wide, shallow bowl

Tenders: Calories: 310; Total Fat (g): 16; Saturated Fat (g): 3; Cholesterol (mg): 99; Sodium (mg): 210; Potassium (mg): 200; Total Carbohydrate (g): 14; Fiber (g): 0; Sugar (g): 0; Protein (g): 25. Content per serving. Assumes 6 servings.

Sauce: Calories: 20; Total Fat (g): 2; Saturated Fat (g): 1; Cholesterol (mg): 0; Sodium (mg): 590; Potassium (mg): 0; Total Carbohydrate (g): 1; Fiber (g): 0; Sugar (g): 1; Protein (g): 0. Content per serving. Assumes 6 servings.

SERVES 4 to 6

EFFORT This is a more involved dish that's best to make on the weekend

ACTIVE PREP 25 to 30 minutes

PAIRING Serve with celery and carrot sticks and beer, such as Omission Lager

SOUTHWEST SALSA

Store-bought salsas may taste great, but too often they're laden with unwanted sodium and preservatives that have no place on the range. This recipe for homemade salsa gives excess salt and nasty chemicals a swift boot while retaining the kick of heat salsa is meant to impart. Easy enough to pull together in less time than it takes to lasso a longhorn, and healthy enough to eat with the reckless abandon of a rodeo clown, this salsa can put a spur into any snacking occasion.

1 Mix ingredients thoroughly in a bowl.

2 Serve with tortilla chips, atop tacos, or alongside any Latin dish.

2 medium heirloom tomatoes, finely chopped

½ yellow onion, finely chopped

2 tbsp. cilantro, finely chopped

1 tsp. smoked paprika

¼ tsp. cumin

¼ tsp. garlic powder

¼ tsp. onion powder

⅛ tsp. sea salt

Juice from 1 lime

Chili powder, to taste

Red pepper flakes, to taste

TIP
Fresh, high quality, flavorful ingredients are key to making this salsa taste great. This recipe accordingly calls for heirloom tomatoes, which tend to be very flavorful.

SERVES 4
EFFORT So little work, so much flavor
ACTIVE PREP 5 to 10 minutes
PAIRING My Marvaritas recipe

Calories: 30; Total Fat (g): 0; Saturated Fat (g): 0; Cholesterol (mg): 0; Sodium (mg): 60; Potassium (mg): 200; Total Carbohydrate (g): 7; Fiber (g): 1; Sugar (g): 4; Protein (g): 1. Content per serving. Assumes 4 servings.

ESPINACAS CON GARBANZOS

The history of Andalucía, Spain, is defined by successive waves of culture – Roman, Moorish, and Christian – each contributing to the current (delicious) state of Andalucían food. A great example of the culinary magic is this dish from Sevilla. Light yet satisfying, espinacas con garbanzos is perfect as an appetizer to be shared among friends, or it can be enjoyed on its own as a lunch entree when eaten with gluten-free bagel chips or crackers. When has history ever been so appetizing?

1 Heat olive oil in a large, deep non-stick skillet over medium to medium-high heat. Add onion and garlic and sauté until onion is soft, about 3 minutes.

2 Add tomato, paprika, cumin, salt, and garbanzo beans. Continue to cook over medium to medium-high heat, stirring frequently, until tomatoes begin to fall apart and garbanzo beans are heated through, about 5 minutes.

3 Stir in spinach and cook until spinach leaves are just wilted. Remove from heat and scoop mixture, including juices, into bowls. Serve immediately.

4 tbsp. extra virgin olive oil

1 yellow onion, thinly sliced

6 garlic cloves, minced

1 small, ripe tomato, peeled and quartered (see "Encore" section for peeling instructions)

2 tsp. smoked paprika

1 tsp. cumin

¼ tsp. salt

15 oz. canned garbanzo beans, drained and rinsed

12 oz. baby spinach, stems removed

Gluten-free crackers or bagel chips (optional)

SERVES 4 to 6
EFFORT Easy enough for a weekday
ACTIVE PREP 15 to 20 minutes
PAIRING Sweet iced tea

TIP

For a show-stealer appetizer at parties, serve with gluten-free bagel chips like Glutino Original Bagel Chips.

Calories: 190; Total Fat (g): 11; Saturated Fat (g): 1; Cholesterol (mg): 0; Sodium (mg): 340; Potassium (mg): 440; Total Carbohydrate (g): 17; Fiber (g): 6; Sugar (g): 2; Protein (g): 6. Content per serving. Assumes 6 servings.

FRIED CALAMARI WITH CHIPOTLE AIOLI

Is there ever a time fried calamari doesn't sound great? Not for me. Happily, this easy preparation for gluten-free fried calamari makes squid fritters an anytime delight. Crispy and light, this treat is great for sharing at home with a bottle of wine or as an appetizer for guests. Paprika and thyme provide subtle seasoning that finishes perfectly with my chipotle aioli, while gluten-free breadcrumbs give these calamari a pleasant crunch. Wouldn't some fried calamari be great right now?

CHIPOTLE AIOLI

¼ cup mayonnaise

1 tbsp. fresh-squeezed lime juice

1 small garlic clove, minced

1 tsp. chipotle chili in adobo sauce, finely minced

1 tsp. chives, finely chopped

½ tsp. ground black pepper

¼ tsp. cumin

¼ tsp. smoked paprika

¼ tsp. or less salt

CALAMARI

1 cup canola oil

½ cup gluten-free breadcrumbs

½ cup gluten-free all-purpose flour

½ tsp. ground black pepper

¼ tsp. smoked paprika

¼ tsp. thyme

¼ tsp. or less salt

1 lb. calamari, mantle sliced into ½-inch rings

1 lemon, quartered

SERVES 4 to 6
EFFORT Medium level
ACTIVE PREP 35 to 40 minutes
PAIRING Michelle Brut

1 In a small bowl, mix together chipotle aioli ingredients. Cover and refrigerate until ready to serve.

2 Heat canola oil in a large, deep skillet over medium to medium-high heat. Place a plate lined with paper towels nearby.

3 While oil heats, whisk together breadcrumbs, flour, pepper, paprika, thyme, and salt in a wide, shallow bowl.

4 Working in batches, dredge calamari in flour mixture, then cook in oil for 4 to 5 minutes, being careful not to overcook calamari (which will turn it rubbery). Place cooked calamari on paper towel-lined plate to drain.

5 Serve while still hot with chipotle aioli and lemon wedges.

Calamari: Calories: 220; Total Fat (g): 11; Saturated Fat (g): 1; Cholesterol (mg): 176; Sodium (mg): 110; Potassium (mg): 200; Total Carbohydrate (g): 17; Fiber (g): 1; Sugar (g): 0; Protein (g): 13. Content per serving. Assumes 6 servings.

Aioli: Calories: 70; Total Fat (g): 7; Saturated Fat (g): 1; Cholesterol (mg): 7; Sodium (mg): 150; Potassium (mg): 0; Total Carbohydrate (g): 1; Fiber (g): 0; Sugar (g): 0; Protein (g): 0. Content per serving. Assumes 6 servings.

ASPARAGUS WITH SPANISH JAMON

Just snap, wrap, and bake – it's that easy to make this delectable dish that is at once salty and sweet, crispy and tender, healthy and succulent. Vitamin-packed asparagus pairs magically with the intensity of Spanish jamón and sweetness of honey. The result is a dish that conjures exotic Andalucían landscapes with minimal effort and has enough adaptability to hold its own alongside most entrees. I especially recommend this dish as accompaniment to fish or my Spanish Tortilla.

1 lb. fresh asparagus spears, ends snapped off

3 to 4 shaved slices Jamón Serrano, cut lengthwise into 3-by-4-inch strips

2 tsp. extra virgin olive oil

Ground black pepper

Honey

1 Preheat oven to 450 degrees.

2 Line a baking sheet with foil and place asparagus spears on baking sheet.

3 Wrap a jamón slice around each spear. To wrap, begin near the base of asparagus and spiral jamón up the stalk, allowing the edges of meat to overlap slightly.

4 Drizzle olive oil over asparagus and rub to coat. Season to taste with black pepper. Bake for 15 minutes or until ham is crispy and tips of spears are slightly browned.

5 Remove asparagus from oven, drizzle with honey to taste (about 1 tbsp. works well), and allow to rest at room temperature for 5 minutes before serving.

SERVES 4
EFFORT Easy after a long day
ACTIVE PREP 5 to 10 minutes
PAIRING Tatometer Kick-On Ranch Riesling

TIP

Omit honey and substitute garlic aioli as a dipping sauce for savory preparation. (See my Blackened Halibut for aioli recipe.)

Calories: 90; Total Fat (g): 4; Saturated Fat (g): 1; Cholesterol (mg): 8; Sodium (mg): 280; Potassium (mg): 230; Total Carbohydrate (g): 9; Fiber (g): 2; Sugar (g): 6; Protein (g): 7. Content per serving. Assumes 4 servings.

SALMOREJO

I'm surely not the only woman who's traveled to the Mediterranean and been swept off her feet by a passionate romance. However, the romance I found took the form of salmorejo, a creamy tomato soup. This pseudo-soup is velvety and luxuriant, and its flavors are so fresh and intense that you can easily lose yourself to a bowl's advances. Spaniards top salmorejo with hardboiled egg and jamón, which complement the tomatoes' acidity and impart additional color to this sensuous dish.

1 Fill a medium-sized bowl with lukewarm water and a dash of salt. Soak bread pieces in water for 30 minutes. Remove bread from water, squeeze out excess water, and set aside.

2 In a deep skillet or medium-sized pot, combine tomatoes with 2 tbsp. olive oil and garlic. Cook over medium-high heat until tomatoes have begun falling apart, about 15 minutes.

3 Transfer tomatoes and bread to a food processor or blender and pulse. Gradually add olive oil and continue pulsing until mixture is creamy.

4 Pour salmorejo into serving bowls and top each bowl with bacon and hard-boiled egg. Serve immediately with ground black pepper on the side for seasoning.

¼ tsp. salt plus extra for soaking bread

2 to 3 slices day-old, gluten-free bread, broken into large pieces

½ cup extra virgin olive oil + 2 tbsp.

3 to 4 large heirloom tomatoes, peeled and chopped (see "Encore" section for peeling instructions)

2 garlic cloves, minced

2 to 3 slices crispy bacon, crumbled

1 hard-boiled egg, crumbled

Ground black pepper

SERVES 6 to 8
EFFORT I prefer to make this on a weekend
ACTIVE PREP 25 to 30 minutes
PAIRING Sweet iced tea for lunch and Daura Damm for dinner

TIP This dish is best served at room temperature but can also be covered, refrigerated, and served chilled.

Calories: 240; Total Fat (g): 20; Saturated Fat (g): 3; Cholesterol (mg): 29; Sodium (mg): 150; Potassium (mg): 240; Total Carbohydrate (g): 13; Fiber (g): 1; Sugar (g): 5; Protein (g): 3. Content per serving. Assumes 8 servings.

BUENOS NACHOS

Nachos are unlikely to make health-food lists, and rightfully so. With high fat and processed cheese additives, nachos leave little room for wholesomeness. Which is unfortunate because, unhealthy as they may be, nachos go hand-in-hand with college football. Enter my quinoa nachos. This recipe calls on red quinoa for its health benefits and rejects nacho cheese. Tangy flavors and creamy-crispy textures remain, but nasty stuff is gone. Say *adios* to unhealthy nachos; say *buenos nachos* instead!

4 servings tortilla chips, about 40 chips

Aged Gouda or lactose-free cheddar, grated

1 cup dry red quinoa, rinsed

2 cups low-sodium vegetable stock

2 tsp. smoked paprika

1 tsp. cumin

½ tsp. chili powder

½ tsp. garlic powder

½ tsp. ground black pepper

2 tsp. canola oil

1 jalapeño pepper, diced

1 red bell pepper, diced

1 small sweet yellow onion, diced

2 garlic cloves, minced

15 oz. canned black beans, rinsed and drained

1 small ripe organic tomato, diced

1 ripe avocado, diced (optional)

1 Preheat oven to 375 degrees.

2 Place tortilla chips on foil baking pan. Sprinkle grated cheese on chips. Set aside.

3 Prepare quinoa according to package instructions, using vegetable stock as the liquid in which it cooks. Once quinoa has begun cooking, stir paprika, cumin, chili powder, garlic powder, and pepper into quinoa. Cover and continue cooking.

4 In a large skillet, heat canola oil over medium to medium-high heat. Add jalapeño, bell pepper, onion, and garlic. Sauté until onions are softened and translucent, about 5 to 7 minutes.

5 Once quinoa has cooked, stir in black beans as well as sauteed jalapeño pepper, bell pepper, onion, and garlic. Let stand.

6 Bake nachos until cheese has melted but before it begins to bubble, about 3 to 5 minutes.

7 Remove nachos from oven, top with quinoa mixture, diced tomato, and avocado. Serve immediately.

SERVES 6 to 8
EFFORT Perfect for Saturdays
ACTIVE PREP 25 to 35 minutes
PAIRING My Prickly Pear Margaritas

Calories: 280; Total Fat (g): 10; Saturated Fat (g): 2; Cholesterol (mg): 0; Sodium (mg): 180; Potassium (mg): 220; Total Carbohydrate (g): 40; Fiber (g): 7; Sugar (g): 4; Protein (g): 9. Content per serving. Assumes 8 servings.

TIP......................

For low-lactose preparation, I recommend using Old Amsterdam Premium Aged Gouda, available at Trader Joe's. Use Daiya Cheddar Shreds for Vegan prep.

MONTEREY FRITTERS

My husband's acceptance of his sensitivity to gluten and lactose came haltingly. He didn't want to give up the dishes he could no longer eat, including foods he ate sparingly like fried mozzarella sticks. So I decided to create a slightly different take on the dish, substituting in lactose-free Monterey Jack and using gluten-free breadcrumbs and flour. Crispy, creamy, indulgent, and safe to eat, these fritters pack great flavor with no lactose and no gluten – a perfect snack when some variety is in order.

½ cup gluten-free breadcrumbs

½ cup gluten-free all-purpose flour

1 tsp. dried thyme

Smoked paprika

Cayenne pepper (optional)

Extra virgin olive oil

8 oz. lactose-free Monterey Jack, sliced into ¼-inch thick wedges

1 egg, lightly beaten in a shallow bowl

1 Combine breadcrumbs, flour, thyme, and a dash of smoked paprika (or cayenne pepper for extra kick) in a shallow bowl. Cover a large plate with paper towel and place beside stovetop.

2 Pour olive oil into a large, non-stick skillet until the oil is about ¼ inch deep. Heat olive oil over low to medium-low heat until shimmering but not smoking.

3 Working in batches, dredge cheese wedges first through egg and then in breadcrumbs and flour, ensuring that all sides of cheese are coated in batter. Place cheese slices in oil and cook until outsides are crisp and browned (about 30 to 45 seconds per side, depending on strength of the heat source).

4 Place cooked cheese wedges on paper towel to drain excess oil. Let cool slightly and serve with marinara sauce on side for dipping.

SERVES 4 to 6

EFFORT Easy enough to make any time

ACTIVE PREP 20 to 25 minutes

PAIRING Irony Pinot Noir, which, like Monterey Jack cheese, hails from Monterey, California

TIP

Use Follow Your Heart Vegan Gourmet Monterey Jack for vegan prep. For low-lactose prep, use Manchego Añejo cheese in place of lactose-free cheese. Use medium to medium-high heat when cooking Manchego Añejo fritters.

Calories: 210; Total Fat (g): 15; Saturated Fat (g): 1; Cholesterol (mg): 36; Sodium (mg): 210; Potassium (mg): 10; Total Carbohydrate (g): 16; Fiber (g): 3; Sugar (g): 0; Protein (g): 3. Content per serving. Assumes 6 servings.

HOMESTYLE MARINARA SAUCE

When I want to wow my guests with a fresh, zesty dipping sauce, this is my go-to recipe. While it takes a bit more effort than popping open a jar of store-bought marinara sauce, I find the work is well worth the extra satisfaction. Serve this dipping sauce with fried calamari or use it as pizza sauce. I like to make my marinara on a cool day in fall or winter. Its sweet, garlicky smell and hint of spice warm the body and soul. This sauce goes great with my Monterey Fritters.

1 In a large non-stick skillet, heat ½ cup olive oil over medium heat. Once heated, add garlic and chilies and stir until fragrant, about 30 seconds.

2 Add tomatoes and sugar to skillet and stir. Season with salt and pepper to taste. Continue cooking over medium to medium-high heat until tomatoes start to fall apart, about 10 to 15 minutes.

3 Remove tomato mixture from heat and pour contents into a food processor. Process until ingredients are chopped. Slowly add remaining (2 tbsp.) olive oil and continue processing until smooth.

4 Let sauce stand at room temperature up to 2 hours before serving. Alternatively, cover and refrigerate sauce until ready to serve.

½ cup extra virgin olive oil + 2 tbsp.

3 garlic cloves, thinly sliced or minced

2 dried red chilies, chopped and seeds removed

4 heirloom tomatoes, peeled and chopped

½ tsp. granulated sugar (optional; omit for Paleo preparation)

Sea salt

Ground black pepper

SERVES 4 to 6
EFFORT Involved enough that I tend to make on special occasions
ACTIVE PREP 25 to 35 minutes
PAIRING My Monterey Fritters or Fried Calamari recipes

TIP

If you don't have any red chilies on hand, substitute ¼ tsp. red pepper flakes.

Calories: 180; Total Fat (g): 18; Saturated Fat (g): 2; Cholesterol (mg): 0; Sodium (g): 20; Potassium (g): 200; Total Carbohydrate (g): 6; Fiber (g): 1; Sugar (g): 4; Protein (g): 1. Content per serving. Assumes 6 servings.

TRUFFLE POPCORN

Whenever I crave gourmet flavor without the gourmet price tag, I go to my truffle popcorn. It can turn any evening from one fit for the Razzies to Oscar-winning. This recipe brings satisfying truffle taste to an easy-to-make and even easier-to-eat movie snack. Simply pop some kernels on the stove and top it off with truffle-infused olive oil and truffle salt. The result is three-dimensional flavor in an IMAX-worthy rendition of popcorn. And the award for best dish in a supporting role goes to...

½ cup organic popping corn, popped in olive oil

3 tbsp. extra virgin olive oil

Black truffle flavored extra virgin olive oil

Himalayan salt with truffles

1 Drizzle popped corn with truffle-flavored olive oil and toss to coat.

2 Sprinkle with Himalayan salt with truffles. Serve immediately.

SERVES 4

EFFORT Easy enough to make during movie preview trailers

ACTIVE PREP 5 to 10 minutes

PAIRING My Balsamic Spritzer recipe

TP

Use Trader Joe's Black Truffle Flavored Extra Virgin Olive Oil and Trader Joe's Himalayan Salt with Truffles.

Calories: 180; Total Fat (g): 12; Saturated Fat (g): 2; Cholesterol (mg): 0; Sodium (mg): 110; Potassium (mg): 0; Total Carbohydrate (g): 17; Fiber (g): 2; Sugar (g): 0; Protein (g): 3. Content per serving. Assumes 4 servings.

ENTREES

My entrées are one part simplicity and one part gourmet. They reflect my years working and experimenting in the kitchen while simultaneously leading a hectic lifestyle (i.e., first as a full-time consultant, then as a graduate student, and finally as an entrepreneur). All derive from my love for tasting food anywhere I travel and my desire to replicate those gourmet flavors without gluten or lactose.

Most of my entrée recipes share a theme of simplicity of preparation, while others involve a bit more work but richly reward the effort. Every recipe, of course, is delicious and healthy – the way to Live Luxe Gluten Free.

SPICED SALMON WITH CURRY DIP

My father-in-law worked in hospitality. Perhaps because of that experience, or maybe because he was born with it, he had a gift for entertaining and hosted fantastic dinner parties. He made it look effortless. At last, he shared one of his secrets – this recipe – with me. It was his standby for gatherings, and it tastes like a high-end restaurant entrée without the price or fuss. This dish is a staple in my kitchen and elicits the enthusiasm of my father-in-law's guests when I serve it now.

SALMON

1 lb. wild-caught salmon fillet (King, Coho, and Sockeye all work well for this recipe; though, if available, I recommend King)

1 tsp. kosher salt or sea salt

1 tsp. ground black pepper

½ tsp. cumin

½ tsp. coriander

½ tsp. allspice

Extra virgin olive oil

1 lemon, quartered

CURRY DIP

¼ cup mayonnaise

1 to 2 tsp. yellow curry powder

....

SERVES 4
EFFORT Perfect for a work night
ACTIVE PREP 10 minutes
PAIRING Melville Pinot Noir or Belle Glos Meiomi Pinot Noir

1 Preheat oven to 400 degrees and line a baking sheet with foil. Place salmon fillet on sheet, skin side down.

2 Mix salmon spices in a small bowl and set aside.

3 Lightly coat salmon with olive oil. Sprinkle seasoning mixture on top of salmon (season to liking; depending on the shape of fillet, you may not need all the seasoning).

4 Bake until fully cooked but still moist, about 15 to 20 minutes.

5 While fish bakes, mix curry dip ingredients in a small bowl.

6 When salmon has finished baking, remove from oven and let rest for a couple of minutes. Serve with fresh sliced lemon and curry dip on the side. Salmon and curry may be refrigerated and served chilled.

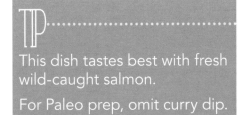

TIP
This dish tastes best with fresh wild-caught salmon.
For Paleo prep, omit curry dip.

Salmon: Calories: 230; Total Fat (g): 13; Saturated Fat (g): 3; Cholesterol (mg): 72; Sodium (mg): 500; Potassium (mg): 520; Total Carbohydrate (g): 0; Fiber (g): 0; Sugar (g): 0; Protein (g): 28. Content per serving. Assumes 4 servings.

Dip: Calories: 100; Total Fat (g): 11; Saturated Fat (g): 2; Cholesterol (mg): 90; Sodium (mg): 0; Potassium (mg): 0; Total Carbohydrate (g): 0; Fiber (g): 0; Sugar (g): 0; Protein (g): 0. Content per serving. Assumes 4 servings.

CARAMELIZED PEAR AND FIG PIZZA

This recipe is my own spin on the baked pear and Brie sandwich served at The Farm of Beverly Hills. I first ate at The Farm with my husband when we were dating and, while I'm sure we had fun on the date, what I really remember about our outing was the baked pear and Brie! My recipe replaces Brie with lactose-free Monterey Jack and adds flavors courtesy of bacon, fig butter, and OJ. Serve this dish to wow guests from any zip code, including 90210.

1 Preheat oven to 375 degrees.

2 Warm butter in a large non-stick skillet over medium heat. Once butter has melted, add brown/palm sugar. Stir until sugar has dissolved, about 2 minutes. Add sliced pears to skillet and cook until pears are slightly softened, about 2 minutes, then add onion and cook for another 5 minutes, stirring occasionally

3 Add orange juice, honey, black pepper, and salt to skillet. Continue cooking mixture over medium heat, stirring occasionally, until most of the liquid has evaporated, about 5 minutes. Remove skillet from heat and set aside.

4 Spread a thin layer of fig butter on each pizza crust, leaving about 1 centimeter around the perimeter of the crust unbuttered. Top buttered portion of crust with evenly-spaced slices of cheese.

5 Place pizzas on top rack of oven and bake for 7 minutes or until edges of crust and cheese are slightly browned.

6 When about 2 minutes of cooking time remain, sprinkle bacon and walnuts atop pizzas, then continue baking. Once pizzas are ready, remove from oven, sprinkle with arugula leaves and then spread pear and onion mixture on top of pizzas. Slice and serve immediately.

Calories: 370; Total Fat (g): 23; Saturated Fat (g): 2; Cholesterol (mg): 3; Sodium (mg): 570; Potassium (mg): 110; Total Carbohydrate (g): 38; Fiber (g): 6; Sugar (g): 14; Protein (g): 7. Content per serving. Assumes 6 servings.

2 tbsp. lactose-free butter

2 tbsp. brown sugar or palm sugar

2 Bosc pears cut into ¼-inch thick slices

½ sweet yellow onion, thinly sliced

⅛ cup orange juice

1 tsp. honey

½ tsp. ground black pepper

Pinch of salt

Fig butter

2 gluten-free pizza crusts, such as Udi's Thin & Crispy Pizza Crusts

10 oz. lactose-free Monterey Jack, cut into ¼-inch thick slices (slice enough to cover pizza crust, about 10 slices per pizza)

2 slices bacon, cooked and chopped

1 handful chopped walnuts

1 handful arugula

SERVES 4 to 6

EFFORT Don't try this on a weeknight

ACTIVE PREP 35 minutes

PAIRING A Spanish red wine, such as Torres Celeste Crianza from Ribera del Duero

ASIAN FRIED CHICKEN

For those eating gluten-free, most fried chicken is off limits. Which makes it no surprise that, despite never being a fried chicken fan beforehand, it became a food my husband regularly said he missed once gluten was gone. So I developed this recipe. The first time my husband tasted it, the expression on his face was first mirthful, then maniacal. I had to guard my plate from his delirium, but he hasn't missed fried chicken since. Make this dish for guaranteed maniacal delight.

½ cup gluten-free all-purpose flour

½ cup gluten-free breadcrumbs

1 tsp. ground black pepper

½ tsp. salt

½ tsp. smoked paprika

¼ tsp. red pepper flakes

1 cup canola oil

1 lb. boneless, skinless chicken breast or tenders, cut into 1-inch cubes

1 egg, lightly beaten in a wide, shallow bowl

1½ cups dry Jasmine rice, prepared according to package instructions

Sweet chili sauce

¼ cup green onion, chopped

1 tbsp. toasted sesame seeds

1 Mix flour, breadcrumbs, pepper, salt, paprika, and red pepper flakes in a wide, shallow bowl and set aside.

2 In a large, deep skillet, heat oil over medium-high heat. Once oil begins to shimmer, working in batches, dredge chicken in egg and then in flour mixture. Place coated chicken in skillet and cook until outsides of chicken are golden brown and meat is cooked through, about 5 to 7 minutes per piece. Flip chicken with tongs halfway through cooking time.

3 Place cooked chicken pieces on a plate lined with paper towels to drain. When ready to serve, place chicken atop rice on serving plates.

4 Heat chili sauce in microwave on high for 30 to 40 seconds. Drizzle chicken and rice with chili sauce and sprinkle with green onion and sesame seeds. Serve immediately.

TIP
I recommend Trader Joe's Sweet Chili Sauce for this recipe.

SERVES 4 to 6
EFFORT Simple enough for a weeknight
ACTIVE PREP 25 to 30 minutes
PAIRING Omission IPA

Calories: 400; Total Fat (g): 12; Saturated Fat (g): 2; Cholesterol (mg): 99; Sodium (mg): 290; Potassium (mg): 210; Total Carbohydrate (g): 42; Fiber (g): 1; Sugar (g): 4; Protein (g): 27. Content per serving. Assumes 6 servings.

IBERIAN SALMON PASTA

While living in Madrid I enjoyed an outstanding variety of foods, including fresh fish. But it was almost impossible to get fresh wild-caught salmon. I eventually tried frozen wild-caught fillets from the supermarket, which, though of good quality, didn't lend themselves to the simple preparation I typically used. So I created this recipe. Pimienton dulce and chorizo infuse the flavors of Madrid, while the use of frozen fillets makes including salmon in the regular rotation economical and easy.

1 In a small bowl, combine paprika, cumin, pepper, salt, and chili powder, if using. Set aside.

2 Heat olive oil in a skillet over medium-low heat. Add red pepper, garlic, and chorizo to skillet. Increase heat to medium and sauté until chorizo is slightly hardened and beginning to brown around the edges, about 2 minutes.

3 Add salmon to skillet and continue sautéing over medium heat until salmon is almost cooked through, about 5 minutes. Add spices to skillet and continue sautéing until salmon is coated in seasoning and thoroughly cooked.

4 Serve salmon and chorizo mixture atop spaghetti. Top with cheese, fresh-squeezed lemon, a drizzle of olive oil, and a sprinkling of paprika and black pepper.

2 tbsp. pimienton dulce (i.e., sweet smoked paprika)

1 tsp. cumin

1 tsp. ground black pepper

½ tsp. salt

¼ tsp. chili powder (optional)

2 tbsp. extra virgin olive oil

1 red bell pepper, diced

3 to 4 garlic cloves, minced

¼ cup chorizo, about ½ link, cut into chunks

1 lb. frozen, wild-caught salmon, thawed and cut into 1-inch chunks with skins and any gray meat removed

1 lb. dry gluten-free spaghetti, prepared according to package instructions

Lactose-free Swiss cheese, grated

1 lemon, sliced into wedges

SERVES 4 to 6
EFFORT Easy enough to make any day of the week
ACTIVE PREP 15 to 20 minutes
PAIRING Pago de los Capellanes Joven Roble from Ribera del Duero

Calories: 460; Total Fat (g): 14; Saturated Fat (g): 2; Cholesterol (mg): 50; Sodium (mg): 220; Potassium (mg): 380; Total Carbohydrate (g): 59; Fiber (g): 3; Sugar (g): 1; Protein (g): 25. Content per serving. Assumes 6 servings.

TIP

Aged, grated Parmesan can be substituted for Swiss cheese for low-lactose preparation.

WHITE CHILI

Borrowing its name from the recipe's chief ingredients, my white chili is a milder alternative to traditional chili. It won't leave you feeling overly full like a heartier, meat-based chili can, but it also doesn't skimp on the coziness chili is so good for. It's a dish I like to make on a Sunday afternoon in winter and enjoy for lunch during the week since it's energizing and great fuel for a workout. I know my white chili is at its creamiest when the quinoa has soaked up most of the liquid in the pot.

2 tsp. extra virgin olive oil

1 red pepper, diced

1 sweet yellow onion, diced

2 cloves garlic, minced or crushed

1¼ tsp. cumin

½ tsp. chili powder

½ tsp. smoked paprika

½ tsp. salt

½ tsp. ground black pepper

1 cup white quinoa, rinsed

2 cups low-sodium vegetable broth

15 oz. canned pinto beans, drained and rinsed

15 oz. canned white kidney beans, drained and rinsed

1 cup frozen corn

Lactose-free, vegan shredded cheddar or aged cheddar, grated (optional)

1 Heat olive oil in a large stockpot over medium-low heat and add red pepper, onion, and garlic. Sauté until ingredients are soft, about 5 minutes.

2 Stir in cumin, chili powder, paprika, salt, and pepper. Heat until fragrant.

3 Add quinoa and vegetable broth, turn heat to high, and bring to a boil.

4 Once boiling, add beans and corn and return to boil. When mixture reaches boil, lower heat, cover, and simmer until most of the liquid is absorbed, about 25 to 30 minutes. Serve topped with shredded cheese as desired.

....

SERVES 4 to 6

EFFORT Easy enough to make on a weeknight

ACTIVE PREP 20 to 25 minutes

PAIRING Bedrock Wine Co.'s Compagni Portis Vineyard Heirloom from Sonoma Valley, California

Calories: 270; Total Fat (g): 7; Saturated Fat (g): 1; Cholesterol (mg): 0; Sodium (mg): 410; Potassium (mg): 550; Total Carbohydrate (g): 45; Fiber (g): 8; Sugar (g): 6; Protein (g): 10. Content per serving. Assumes 6 servings.

TIP ....
Try adding a dollop of lactose-free sour cream to a serving of chili for extra creaminess. I call this treatment the "White Out."

BLACKENED HALIBUT WITH GARLIC AIOLI

Blackened halibut is such a fantastic meal. Unfortunately, the dish can be expensive at restaurants, and too many recipes call for ingredients that overwhelm halibut's natural charms. When in season, Pacific halibut is a succulent, meaty, and clean-tasting fish whose flavor profile is fully brought to life when it's blackened. The juices are locked in, and carefully selected spices complement the meat's character. A squeeze of lemon and some garlic aioli finish the dish off perfectly.

1 Combine aioli ingredients in a small bowl. Cover and refrigerate until ready to serve.

2 For halibut seasoning, combine garlic powder, oregano, thyme, chili powder, black pepper, paprika, and salt in a small bowl. Mix well. Rub seasoning mixture over halibut fillets, coating evenly. Fillets should be coated thoroughly enough that their white color isn't visible. Set aside.

3 Heat butter in a cast iron skillet over medium heat. Once butter is melted, place fillets in skillet and cook for about 3 minutes per side on all six sides (about 15 to 20 minutes total), until fillets are browned and firm all around. (Note: halibut fillets often are thick, almost block-like, which is why cooking on all sides is recommended.)

4 When ready, remove fillets from skillet and serve immediately with a slice of lemon and garlic aioli.

GARLIC AIOLI
¼ cup mayonnaise

1 garlic clove, crushed

Juice from ¼ lemon

¼ tsp. lemon pepper

⅛ tsp. salt

BLACKENED HALIBUT
2 tbsp. garlic powder

1 tbsp. dried oregano

1 tbsp. dried thyme

1 tbsp. chili powder

1 tbsp. ground black pepper

2½ tsp. smoked paprika

1 tsp. salt

1 lb. fresh, wild-caught Pacific halibut fillets, cut into 4 oz. servings, skin left on

2 tbsp. lactose-free butter

1 lemon, sliced into 4 wedges

Halibut: Calories: 180; Total Fat (g): 7; Saturated Fat (g): 2; Cholesterol (mg): 68; Sodium (mg): 580; Potassium (mg): 600; Total Carbohydrate (g): 0; Fiber (g): 0; Sugar (g): 0; Protein (g): 25. Content per serving. Assumes 4 servings.

Aioli: Calories: 100; Total Fat (g): 11; Saturated Fat (g): 2; Cholesterol (mg): 10; Sodium (mg): 150; Potassium (mg): 0; Total Carbohydrate (g): 0; Fiber (g): 0; Sugar (g): 0; Protein (g): 0. Content per serving. Assumes 4 servings.

SERVES 4

EFFORT Easy enough to make after a long day at work. What a treat!

ACTIVE PREP 20 to 25 minutes

PAIRING Citrusy white wine such as Chenin Blanc, Gewürztraminer, or Pinot Blanc

QUINOA STUFFED PEPPERS

When I was growing up, my parents would make stuffed green peppers with mashed potatoes. Sweet aromas of peppers cooking with meat and tomato would suffuse the house – a prelude of the meal to come – and I'd scarf things down by mixing the peppers and their sauce with the mashed potatoes. Just like they used to at my parents' house, alluring scents fill my kitchen when I make this terrific comfort food. Its mild flavors and gentle warmth make it terrific on cool, fall evenings.

1 Cut tops off of peppers and core (like you would a Halloween pumpkin for carving). Save pepper tops.

2 Mix rice with quinoa and pork sausage and stir in pepper, paprika, salt, nutmeg, coriander, garlic powder, and onion powder.

3 Stuff peppers with quinoa, sausage, and rice mixture. Replace tops.

4 Place peppers in a large stockpot and pour tomato juice over them. Bring mixture to a boil, then reduce heat to medium-low. Cover and let simmer for about 80 minutes.

5 Serve immediately and ladle extra tomato sauce on top of peppers.

4 to 6 bell peppers (use red peppers for sweeter palates)

½ cup dry rice, prepared according to package instructions

1 cup dry red quinoa, cooked in water

½ lb. pork sausage, casings removed and insides crumbled

½ tsp. ground black pepper

½ tsp. smoked paprika

½ tsp. salt

¼ tsp. nutmeg

⅛ tsp. coriander

Dash of garlic powder

Dash of onion powder

64 oz. tomato/vegetable juice blend

SERVES 6 to 8
EFFORT Definitely something to make on the weekend
ACTIVE PREP 25 to 30 minutes
PAIRING Hard apple cider or a red wine, such as Zinfandel or Chianti Classico

Calories: 350; Total Fat (g): 9; Saturated Fat (g): 2; Cholesterol (mg): 19; Sodium (mg): 430; Potassium (mg): 670; Total Carbohydrate (g): 55; Fiber (g): 7; Sugar (g): 12; Protein (g): 14. Content per serving. Assumes 8 servings.

TIP

I recommend using Trader Joe's Low Sodium Garden Patch juice for vegetable juice blend.

SPANISH TORTILLA

¼ cup extra virgin olive oil + 2 to 3 tbsp.

8 to 10 new potatoes, thinly sliced

1 yellow onion, thinly sliced

1 small to medium eggplant, thinly sliced

6 large eggs, beaten in a large bowl

Salt

Ground black pepper

SERVES 6 to 8

EFFORT Save this for a day when you really feel like dedicating your energy to cooking

ACTIVE PREP 45 minutes to 1 hour

PAIRING Freshly squeezed orange juice or my Tinto de Verano recipe

Calories: 250; Total Fat (g): 10; Saturated Fat (g): 2; Cholesterol (mg): 161; Sodium (mg): 120; Potassium (mg): 830; Total Carbohydrate (g): 33; Fiber (g): 5; Sugar (g): 4; Protein (g): 8. Content per serving. Assumes 8 servings.

1 Heat a large non-stick skillet over medium to medium-high heat. Add ¼ cup olive oil to skillet and heat. Once oil is shimmering, add potatoes, onions, and eggplant to skillet and sauté, stirring until potatoes are soft and eggplant is cooked through, about 25 minutes. Remove skillet from heat.

2 Strain potatoes, onion, and eggplant.

3 Season eggs with salt and pepper to taste. Gently stir potato, onion, and eggplant mixture into bowl with eggs and let rest for 10 minutes.

4 While mixture rests, use a wooden spatula to scrape any ingredients stuck to the skillet. Once remnants have been scraped away and discarded, heat skillet over medium-high heat and add 2 to 3 tbsp. of olive oil. Heat olive oil until it is warmed and shimmering but not smoking.

5 Add egg mixture to skillet and use spatula to spread evenly throughout pan. As egg begins to cook, loosen edges with spatula. Shake skillet and rotate occasionally to allow mixture to settle. After egg mixture has cooked for about 5 minutes, place a large plate on top and flip mixture over onto plate (do this over a sink and use an oven mitt, as hot oil may fall out of skillet). Add more olive oil to skillet, if needed, and swirl to coat.

6 Slide tortilla, uncooked side down, back into skillet and continue cooking over medium-high heat. Loosen edges again with spatula and shake and rotate skillet to allow mixture to settle.

7 Once tortilla is cooked through (after about 3 to 5 minutes), remove skillet from heat, transfer tortilla to clean serving plate and allow to rest at room temperature for 10 minutes. Slice into pie-shaped wedges and serve.

A favorite Spanish tapa is tortilla, which, though tedious to make, is worth the effort. Tortilla tastes great served warm or at room temperature, and it can be enjoyed either as a small bite or, if served like quiche, as an entrée. Tortilla can be enhanced by a variety of sauces, including everything from ketchup to garlic aioli. But, of course, tortilla does not need any help in the flavor department and can be enjoyed completely unadorned.

PRETTY, POWERFUL, PASTA

S

This recipe came together when my pantry and fridge were bare. Unable to get to the store, I was limited to tomatoes, broccoli, and Trader Joe's quinoa fusilli pasta. I combined them all then added garlic, olive oil, and anchovies to the mix. The result: a bright and savory meal perfect for spring. This beautiful dish provides greens, omega-3s, lycopene, and ancient grains. Plus, the health benefits of tomatoes and broccoli are magnified when eaten together. Pretty and powerful!

½ head of broccoli, chopped into bite-size florets

2 tbsp. extra virgin olive oil

2 garlic cloves, crushed

2 medium-sized, very ripe heirloom tomatoes, cored and chopped

3 anchovy fillets, chopped

8 oz. dry gluten-free quinoa fusilli pasta, prepared according to package instructions

Ground black pepper

1 Heat a small pot filled with ½ inch water over high heat. When water begins to boil, add broccoli, cover, and cook for 2 minutes. Remove from heat, drain, and set aside.

2 Heat olive oil in a non-stick skillet over medium to medium-high heat for 1 minute. Add garlic and stir until garlic is mixed into oil, being careful not to overcook.

3 Add broccoli, tomatoes, and anchovies to skillet and sauté over medium-high heat for about 5 minutes, or until tomatoes have almost dissolved, broccoli has softened a bit, and tomato-colored liquid has accumulated in the bottom of skillet.

4 Dish pasta into bowls. Pour tomato, broccoli, and anchovy mixture over pasta. Stir and serve immediately. Season with freshly ground black pepper to taste.

SERVES 2 to 3
EFFORT Easy enough to make on a busy weekday
ACTIVE PREP 15 minutes
PAIRING Lemonade if serving for lunch; Chianti Classico if serving for dinner

TIP For this recipe, I recommend using ripened heirloom tomatoes and extra virgin olive oil with provenance from Italy, California, or Spain.

Calories: 390; Total Fat (g): 12; Saturated Fat (g): 2; Cholesterol (mg): 4; Sodium (mg): 200; Potassium (mg): 260; Total Carbohydrate (g): 63; Fiber (g): 3; Sugar (g): 3; Protein (g): 8. Content per serving. Assumes 3 servings.

MACADAMIA-ENCRUSTED MAHI-MAHI

This island-inspired recipe is the perfect way to incorporate fish, nuts, and fruit into one tasty meal. Featuring flavors from Hawaii – macadamias, coconuts, and, of course, mahi-mahi – this dish has more textures than the islands do beaches: macadamia nuts and pan-seared gluten-free flour give this fish a crispy exterior; searing and baking keep the meat tender and flaky; and fruit salsa adds juicy bites of citrus. This is a meal that will have your dinner guests saying "mahalo"!

½ cup macadamia nuts, finely chopped

¼ cup gluten-free all-purpose flour (coconut flour works as well)

¼ to ½ cup coconut milk

2 tbsp. lactose-free butter

1 lb. wild-caught mahi-mahi fillets, thawed if frozen

Sea salt

Ground black pepper

Citrus salsa for topping, such as pineapple mango salsa

1 Preheat oven to 400 degrees.

2 Mix macadamia nuts and flour in a wide, shallow bowl and set beside stovetop. Pour coconut milk in a wide, shallow bowl and place beside nut mixture.

3 Heat butter in a non-stick skillet over medium-high heat.

4 Pat mahi-mahi fillets dry with a paper towel and season with salt and pepper to liking. Dip each fillet first in coconut milk and then in macadamia nut mixture, ensuring entire outside of each fillet is covered with nut mixture.

5 Place fillets in sizzling skillet and cook for 2 minutes per side being careful not to burn the macadamias – they should take on a golden hue but not brown deeply.

6 Place fillets in glass baking dish and bake until cooked through and flaky, about 10 to 15 minutes, depending on the shape of fillets. Top with salsa and serve.

SERVES 4

EFFORT This is easy enough for a weeknight, though I prefer to make it on evenings when I'm not feeling rushed

ACTIVE PREP 15 to 20 minutes

PAIRING Tropical drinks, of course!

Calories: 350; Total Fat (g): 22; Saturated Fat (g): 6; Cholesterol (mg): 107; Sodium (mg): 290; Potassium (mg): 690; Total Carbohydrate (g): 8; Fiber (g): 1; Sugar (g): 1; Protein (g): 28. Content per serving, exclusive of mango salsa. Assumes 4 servings.

To create a homemade citrus-mango salsa, thaw ¼ to ½ cup frozen mango cubes. Dice mango, dice a small amount of red onion, and chop several parsley leaves. Place mango, red onion, and parsley in a small serving dish. Squeeze the juice from ¼ lime over mixture, stir, and serve. Season with salt and pepper to taste.

THAI PORK CURRY

CURRY POWDER

3 tbsp. cumin

2 tbsp. coriander

2 tbsp. turmeric

1½ tbsp. ground black pepper

4 tsp. cloves

1 tsp. cinnamon

1 tsp. nutmeg

CURRY PASTE

5 to 10 dried red Thai chilies, soaked in water for 20 to 25 minutes, reserve water*

5 garlic cloves, chopped

4 to 6 lemongrass stalks, both white and green parts thinly sliced

1 shallot, chopped

2 tsp. shrimp paste

1 tsp. fresh galangal, peeled and chopped

MARINADE

2 lbs. pork shoulder, cut into 3-inch cubes

1 lb. pork belly, cut into 3-inch cubes

4-inch piece fresh ginger, peeled and julienned

½ cup liquid from pickled garlic

5 heads pickled garlic, separated into cloves

3 tbsp. palm sugar

3 tbsp. tamarind concentrate

2 to 4 cups jasmine rice, cooked

1 Mix curry powder ingredients in a bowl and set aside.

2 Place soaked chilies, fresh garlic cloves, lemongrass, shallot, shrimp paste, and galangal in food processor with a small amount (about 6 tbsp.) of water reserved from soaking chilies. Process until smooth. Add more reserved water if needed, processing until a paste is formed.

3 Pour paste into a large bowl containing pork shoulder and pork belly. Rub to coat evenly. Add curry powder, rubbing again to coat. Cover bowl with foil and refrigerate for 1 to 4 hours.

4 Heat a large cast iron skillet over medium-high heat. Cook pork, stirring occasionally, until the outsides of meat are lightly browned, about 8 to 10 minutes total.

5 Place pork and any spice remnants from the skillet in slow cooker. Add ginger, pickled garlic juice, and 3 cups of water. Cook on low heat setting for 10 hours or until pork is tender and breaks apart easily when pulled with a fork.

6 Add pickled garlic heads to slow cooker and continue cooking on low for 2 hours. When pork is finished cooking, stir in palm sugar and tamarind concentrate. Season to taste with salt. Serve with jasmine rice.

SERVES 10 to 12
EFFORT An involved dish to be made on special occasions
ACTIVE PREP 35 to 40 minutes
PAIRING Omission Lager

*1 to 3 chilies = mild; 4 to 7 chilies = medium; 8 to 10 chilies = hot

Calories: 380; Total Fat (g): 30; Saturated Fat (g): 10; Cholesterol (mg): 76; Sodium (mg): 160; Potassium (mg): 330; Total Carbohydrate (g): 9; Fiber (g): 1; Sugar (g): 1; Protein (g): 19. Content per serving, exclusive of rice. Assumes 12 servings.

Pork belly, a cut of meat blessed with an embarrassment of textures and flavors, is at its best when cooked slowly to break down its collagen fibers and served with the juices that yield as it heats. I like pork belly smothered in yellow curry to offset the meat's richness with casual spice. It's a combination so perfect that, once you've tasted it, you'll have trouble believing yellow curry wasn't invented specifically for this porcine paragon.

TIP

Asian markets or stores with large selections of hard-to-find foods, like Whole Foods, are safe bets for finding this recipe's ingredients.

SKILLET Burger & Spunky Sauce

TIP

Dice tomatoes and shred lettuce, then mix into spunky sauce to prevent toppings from sliding.

SKILLET BURGERS 'N SPUNKY SAUCE

This burger recipe pays homage to the burgers served at places like New York City's Shake Shack and California's In-N-Out. Basic, tasty, and the kind of treat that's usually off-limits for those eating gluten- and lactose-free, my Skillet Burgers 'n Spunky Sauce take care of drive-thru cravings with moxie. Spunky sauce adds creaminess and zest to juicy patties, and, if these burgers are devoured over a plate of fries, the juices that escape are the perfect toppings for 'taters. Order up!

1 In a small bowl, whisk together ingredients for spunky sauce. Add salt to taste. Cover and refrigerate until ready to serve.

2 In a large bowl, combine egg, salt, pepper, Worcestershire sauce, garlic powder, and grated onion. Very lightly work mixture into beef until just combined. Gently form 4 to 6 patties using fingers. Don't overwork meat. Form patties slightly larger in circumference than buns. Press centers of patties with thumb to make a ¼-inch depression in the meat.

3 Heat a large cast iron skillet over medium-high heat. While skillet heats, spread a thin layer of Dijon mustard on one side of each burger patty. Cook patties for 2 to 3 minutes per side, to liking. Remove from skillet and drain on plate lined with paper towel. Allow burgers to rest.

4 Sauté sliced onions in skillet with 1 tsp. butter for 2 to 3 minutes. While onions sauté, heat burger buns in skillet, insides facing down, until inside edges are slightly browned, about 2 minutes.

5 Place burgers on bottom halves of buns. Top beef patties with spunky sauce and sautéed onions. Enjoy.

Burgers: Calories: 160; Total Fat (g): 12; Saturated Fat (g): 3; Cholesterol (mg): 81; Sodium (mg): 220; Potassium (mg): 230; Total Carbohydrate (g): 1; Fiber (g): 0; Sugar (g): 0; Protein (g): 14. Content per serving, exclusive of burger buns. Assumes 6 servings.

Sauce: Calories: 70; Total Fat (g): 7; Saturated Fat (g): 1; Cholesterol (mg): 7; Sodium (mg): 90; Potassium (mg): 0; Total Carbohydrate (g): 1; Fiber (g): 0; Sugar (g): 1; Protein (g): 0. Content per serving. Assumes 6 servings.

SPUNKY SAUCE

¼ cup mayonnaise

2 tbsp. yellow onion, diced and sautéed

1 tbsp. ketchup

1 tsp. white vinegar

¼ tsp. Worcestershire sauce

⅛ tsp. dry mustard

Salt

Dash of hot sauce

BURGERS

1 egg, lightly beaten

½ tsp. salt

½ tsp. ground black pepper

¼ tsp. Worcestershire sauce

¼ tsp. garlic powder

¼ medium yellow onion, grated + ¼ thinly sliced for topping

1 lb. 85 percent lean grass-fed beef

Dijon mustard

1 tsp. lactose-free butter

4 gluten-free burger buns

SERVES 4 to 6

EFFORT Easy enough to make any day of the week

ACTIVE PREP 15 to 20 minutes.

PAIRING My Crispy Steak Fries

CASHEW BUTTER STIR-FRY

I used to frequent a Chinese restaurant that served the best breaded and fried peanut chicken entrée – it tasted just like salty peanut butter! I had to replicate the dish on my own. As I experimented with peanut flavors, however, I discovered that cashew butter makes this dish downright magical. So my rendition of peanut stir-fry is actually cashew butter stir-fry! Serve atop steamed rice and you've got a great meal filled with vegetables, protein, and cashew-buttery sweetness.

¼ cup gluten-free breadcrumbs

¼ cup gluten-free all-purpose flour

2 tsp. garlic powder (1 tsp. for flour mixture + 1 tsp. for seasoning)

½ tsp. ground black pepper

¼ tsp. salt

1 head broccoli, chopped into bite-size florets

1 cup shredded carrots

6 tbsp. canola oil

½ lb. boneless, skinless chicken breasts or tenders, cut into 1-inch cubes

1 egg, lightly beaten in a wide, shallow bowl

1 tbsp. lactose-free butter, room temperature

4 tbsp. cashew butter

2 cups dry rice, prepared according to package instructions

1 In a wide, shallow bowl, mix together breadcrumbs, flour, 1 tsp. garlic powder, pepper, and salt. Set beside stovetop.

2 Blanch broccoli and carrots by placing them in boiling water for 1 to 2 minutes. Drain vegetables in colander and run cold water over them.

3 Heat canola oil in a large non-stick wok over medium to medium-high heat. Dredge chicken in egg and then flour mixture. Place dredged chicken in skillet and heat until golden brown, about 5 minutes per side, or 10 minutes total. Place cooked chicken pieces on a plate lined with paper towels. Remove wok from heat and drain excess oil.

4 Stir butter and 1 tsp. garlic powder into cashew butter.

5 Return empty wok to stovetop over low heat. Add chicken and blanched vegetables. Stir in cashew butter mixture until chicken and vegetables are coated. Serve over steamed rice.

SERVES 2 to 4

EFFORT This gets easier with practice but should be reserved for weekends on the first couple of rounds

ACTIVE PREP 30 to 35 minutes

PAIRING Omission Lager

TIP Coconut flour may be used in place of all-purpose flour if desired.

Calories: 390; Total Fat (g): 24; Saturated Fat (g): 3; Cholesterol (mg): 102; Sodium (mg): 230; Potassium (mg): 320; Total Carbohydrate (g): 20; Fiber (g): 2; Sugar (g): 3; Protein (g): 24. Content per serving. Assumes 4 servings.

LATE-SUMMER CRAB GRITS

My mother-in-law's shrimp 'n grits recipe was a long-time favorite before my husband could no longer eat it. Creamy, spicy, and comforting, the dish was perfect on late-summer evenings. I concocted this crab grits recipe that takes its cue from shrimp 'n grits, keeping the creaminess intact while complying with dietary restrictions. With a dash of spice and crab infused with garlic butter, this recipe remains perfect for any late-summer evening.

4 tbsp. lactose-free butter
1 green bell pepper, diced
2 cloves garlic, minced
3 ripe tomatoes, diced
3 scallions, chopped
2 tbsp. diced green chilies
8 oz. wild-caught crabmeat
1½ cups water
1½ cups low-sodium vegetable stock
1 cup Southern-Style grits, dry
¼ cup lactose-free shredded cheddar
½ tsp. ground black pepper
¼ tsp. cayenne pepper

1 In a large non-stick skillet, heat butter over medium heat. Sauté bell pepper and garlic, stirring frequently until garlic is softened, about 3 minutes.

2 Stir in tomatoes, scallions, and green chilies. Continue cooking until tomatoes are softened, about 5 minutes.

3 Stir in crabmeat and continue cooking until ingredients are mixed and crab is warm, 3 to 5 minutes.

4 While crabmeat heats, bring water and vegetable stock to a boil in a medium saucepan. Stir in grits, reduce heat to low, and cook until liquid is absorbed, stirring occasionally, about 5 minutes.

5 When grits are ready, stir crabmeat mixture into grits. Stir in cheddar, black pepper, and cayenne. Add more spice or cheese as desired. Serve immediately.

SERVES 4
EFFORT Easy enough to pull together almost any day of the week
ACTIVE PREP 20 to 25 minutes
PAIRING Sparkling wine, such as Cava, Prosecco, or Champagne

Calories: 340; Total Fat (g): 12; Saturated Fat (g): 3; Cholesterol (mg): 50; Sodium (mg): 450; Potassium (mg): 520; Total Carbohydrate (g): 39; Fiber (g): 4; Sugar (g): 6; Protein (g): 17. Content per serving. Assumes 4 servings.

TIP

When in season, use steamed lobster tail in place of crab-meat for some delicious variety.

CHAMPAGNE SCALLOP RISOTTO

Food can be a lot like music. Just as a down-tempo beat can slow the rhythms of life, so can certain foods make you want to ease your pace and relish the moment – bite by bite. My scallop risotto is one of those foods. Rich, savory, and beautiful, this dish can cause just about anyone to live in the moment and enjoy the comfort of a meal that is sophisticated and healthy. Champagne is a natural accompaniment, but no matter what it's served with, this harmonious dish hits all the right notes.

3 tbsp. lactose-free butter

½ yellow onion, diced

4 oz. crimini mushrooms, sliced

1 cup Arborio rice, dry

½ cup champagne

4 cups low-sodium vegetable broth

6 oz. organic baby spinach, stems removed

¼ cup Parmigiano-Reggiano, aged 12 to 24 months or lactose-free Parmesan, grated

1 lb. jumbo sea scallops, thawed if frozen

Salt

Ground black pepper

1 tbsp. extra virgin olive oil

....

SERVES 3 to 4

EFFORT Best to save for a weekend

ACTIVE PREP 45 to 50 minutes

PAIRING Champagne or sparkling white wine, such as Gloria Ferrer Brut

Calories: 460; Total Fat (g): 14; Saturated Fat (g): 4; Cholesterol (mg): 42; Sodium (mg): 800; Potassium (mg): 740; Total Carbohydrate (g): 49; Fiber (g): 3; Sugar (g): 4; Protein (g): 29. Content per serving. Assumes 4 servings.

1 In a large, deep non-stick skillet, heat 2 tbsp. butter over medium-high heat. When butter starts to sizzle, place onions and mushrooms in skillet and sauté until mushrooms begin to lose their juices and onions are translucent, about 3 to 5 minutes. Add rice and champagne to skillet. Sauté until champagne is absorbed.

2 Gradually stir in vegetable stock, about 1 cup at a time. Allow each cup of stock to be absorbed before adding more (takes about 25 to 30 minutes total).

3 When all of the stock has been added and absorbed, turn heat to medium-low and stir in spinach. Continue stirring until leaves are wilted. Stir in cheese, loosely cover, and set aside.

4 Pat scallops dry and season with salt and pepper on each side to taste.

5 In a separate non-stick skillet, heat 1 tbsp. butter and 1 tbsp. olive oil over medium-high heat. When oil and butter mixture is hot, brown scallops on both flat sides, about 3 to 4 minutes per side. The rounded outside edges of the scallops will look white and opaque when scallops are cooked, and the flat sides will turn a light golden brown. Be careful not to overcook scallops, as they turn rubbery.

6 When scallops are ready, remove from heat promptly and place atop risotto on plates. Add more cheese to the risotto and freshly ground black pepper if desired. Serve immediately.

SWEET POTATO ENCHILADAS

The first time I tried sweet potato enchiladas, I was at a business lunch in downtown Chicago. I wolfed them down in a frenzy of delight. It was utter carnage. While I may not be proud of my behavior at lunch that day, I am proud of my gluten-free and lactose-free version of sweet potato enchiladas. These enchiladas are healthy, great tasting, and exceptionally easy to make. All of which means less fuss in the kitchen and more carnage at the table. Get ready for a frenzy-inducing feast!

1 Mix sour cream and salsa in a small bowl and set aside.

2 Heat a large non-stick skillet over medium heat and add butter. Heat tortillas in pan until they are soft and pliable, about 30 seconds to 1 minute per side.

3 Lay tortillas on a plate and place sweet potato pieces in each shell. Season to liking with chili powder, paprika, cumin, salt, and pepper. Top with sour cream and salsa mixture. Roll tortilla shells closed. Top with extra salsa and devour.

4 tbsp. lactose-free sour cream

2 tbsp. tomatillo salsa

½ tbsp. lactose-free butter

4 soft corn tortillas

2 medium sweet potatoes, cooked and chopped into ½-inch bite-size pieces

Chili powder

Smoked paprika

Cumin

Salt

Ground black pepper

SERVES 2 to 4
EFFORT Very easy
ACTIVE PREP 10 minutes
PAIRING Serve alongside black beans and rice with lemonade in the afternoon or my Marvaritas in the evening

TIP

I recommend Trader José's Salsa Verde from Trader Joe's. Use vegan sour cream for vegan prep.

Calories: 180; Total Fat (g): 7; Saturated Fat (g): 4; Cholesterol (mg): 18; Sodium (mg): 130; Potassium (mg): 260; Total Carbohydrate (g): 26; Fiber (g): 3; Sugar (g): 3; Protein (g): 3. Content per serving. Assumes 4 servings.

INDIAN JALFREZI CHICKEN

It's hard not to love chicken tikka masala. Unfortunately, since masala sauce generally is made with yogurt and cream, finding love in a lactose-free version takes more work than simply ordering takeout. My recipe for at-home Indian relies on lactose-free Jalfrezi sauce and yields a tasty and relatively low-sodium dish that never fails to satisfy. Let the love simmer long and hot with this dish that brings together the spices of India with lactose-free preparation.

1 Heat a large, deep skillet over medium-high heat. Add Jalfrezi sauce, chicken, potatoes, peas, garbanzo beans, and carrots to skillet. Stir until chicken and vegetables are coated in sauce. Once sauce starts to boil, reduce heat to medium, cover, and simmer until chicken is cooked through and potatoes are soft, about 20 minutes. Stir occasionally.

2 Once chicken is cooked through, add coconut milk to skillet, stir, and continue cooking until sauce starts to simmer. Remove from heat.

3 Microwave butter and garlic on high for 10 seconds. Stir.

4 Spread garlic butter on toast and sprinkle with basil leaves. Save some garlic butter to add to Jalfrezi.

5 Stir remaining butter into Jalfrezi. Serve over rice with garlic toast for dipping.

16 oz. Jalfrezi simmer sauce

8 oz. chicken breast, cut into ½-inch cubes

1½ cups new potatoes, peeled and cut into ½-inch bites

½ cup frozen peas

½ cup canned garbanzo beans, rinsed and drained

½ cup shredded carrots

2 tbsp. lactose-free butter

2 garlic cloves, crushed

½ cup low-fat coconut milk

4 slices gluten-free bread, toasted

3 to 4 basil leaves, chopped

1 to 2 cups dry Basmati rice, prepared according to package instructions

TIP

For vegan prep, replace chicken with bite-size cauliflower florets and use Earth Balance Natural Buttery Spread.

Calories: 500; Total Fat (g): 13; Saturated Fat (g): 5; Cholesterol (mg): 31; Sodium (mg): 430; Potassium (mg): 950; Total Carbohydrate (g): 73; Fiber (g): 5; Sugar (g): 8; Protein (g): 19. Content per serving. Assumes 6 servings.

SERVES 4 to 6
EFFORT I tend to make this on evenings when I get home from the office a little early
ACTIVE PREP 25 to 30 minutes
PAIRING Gluten-free lager or a pinot noir, such as Carmel Road Monterey Pinot Noir from California

TIP

If serving this dish for guests, make the grit cakes one day before, cover under pressed plastic wrap, and refrigerate overnight. To prepare grits the next day, pick up the recipe from step 5.

Calories: 360; Total Fat (g): 16; Saturated Fat (g): 7; Cholesterol (mg): 185; Sodium (mg): 570; Potassium (mg): 140; Total Carbohydrate (g): 26; Fiber (g): 2; Sugar (g): 6; Protein (g): 22. Content per serving. Assumes 6 servings.

FAMOUS BBQ SHRIMP AND CHORIZO GRITS

Whenever I dine at a restaurant with a so-called famous dish, I always order it. Maybe I'm a sucker for marketing since these "famous" foods aren't unfailingly great. But every so often – just often enough – they're outstanding. That was the case with BBQ shrimp I ordered on vacation. The shrimp, seasoned with BBQ sauce, rested atop a chorizo grit cake. Delicious. I had to create a lactose-free version, and here it is, perfect as a meal or appetizer. Serve and you'll soon be famous for this delight.

1 Lightly grease a 9-by-11-inch glass baking dish and set aside.

2 Heat a cast iron skillet over medium to medium-high heat. Cook chorizo in skillet until lightly browned, about 5 minutes. Set aside.

3 In a medium saucepan, heat half and half and vegetable stock and bring to a simmer. Stir in grits, set heat to low, and cook, stirring occasionally, until mixture is thick, about 3 to 5 minutes. Season with cayenne pepper and hot sauce to liking. Stir in chorizo.

4 Pour mixture into greased baking dish, press to spread evenly, and cover. Let stand for 30 minutes or until firm.

5 Mix barbecue sauce and ¼ cup half and half in a small bowl and set aside. Mix chili, garlic, and onion powders and pepper and salt in a small bowl and set aside.

6 Rinse and pat shrimp dry. Rub dry seasoning all over shrimp.

7 Slice grits into evenly sized cakes and sprinkle any remaining dry seasoning atop cakes.

8 Heat cast iron skillet over medium-high heat and coat lightly with canola oil. Cook grit cakes in skillet until lightly crisped on the outside, about 2 to 3 minutes per side. Place grits in oven on low temp to keep warm.

9 When grits are finished cooking, keep skillet on medium to medium-high heat and add shrimp, cooking about 1 to 2 minutes per side until cooked through. Place shrimp on top of grit cakes, drizzle with barbecue mixture, and sprinkle with scallions. Serve.

GRITS

Canola oil

1 to 2 chorizo sausage links, cut into small chunks

1½ cups lactose-free half and half

1½ cups low-sodium vegetable stock

1 cup Southern-Style grits

Dash of cayenne pepper

Dash of hot sauce

SHRIMP

4 tbsp. barbecue sauce

¼ cup lactose-free half and half

2 tsp. chili powder

1½ tsp. garlic powder

1 tsp. onion powder

½ tsp. ground black pepper

¼ tsp. salt

1 lb. wild caught shrimp, peeled and deveined

2 to 3 tbsp. scallions, finely chopped

SERVES 4 to 6
EFFORT Involved
ACTIVE PREP 30 minutes
PAIRING Walla Walla red wine, such as Dumas Station Cow Catcher

LEMON AND GARLIC SPICED CHICKEN

There's something incredibly comforting about roasted chicken. This recipe, consoling and easy, is always satisfying when some soothing is needed. With crackling and juicy skin, tender meat, and aromas that can make just about anywhere feel like home, this dish gratifies the senses. Dress it up with French green beans or sautéed mushrooms, or serve with a cold beer and sit outside under starlight. Either way, bring napkins for this succulent, feel-good meal.

10 to 15 new potatoes, quartered into ¾-inch wedges

2 tbsp. extra virgin olive oil

Sea salt

Ground black pepper

4 to 5 lb. whole free-range chicken, rinsed and dried with innards removed

Smoked paprika

Dried rosemary

1 lemon, sliced into 4 wedges

4 garlic cloves, crushed

•••••••••••••••••••••••••••••••

SERVES 6 to 8
ACTIVE PREP 15 minutes
EFFORT Simple but requires over an hour of cooking time
PAIRING Daura Damm or a Pinot Noir, such as Belle Glos Pinot Noir – Clark & Telephone

Calories: 360; Total Fat (g): 14; Saturated Fat (g): 3; Cholesterol (mg): 44; Sodium (mg): 130; Potassium (mg): 1130; Total Carbohydrate (g): 39; Fiber (g): 4; Sugar (g): 2; Protein (g): 19. Content per serving. Assumes 8 servings.

1 Preheat oven to 425 degrees and position rack in middle of oven.

2 Place potatoes in a 9-by-11-inch glass baking dish and toss with 1 tbsp. olive oil. Season to liking with salt and pepper and push seasoned potatoes to perimeter of dish. Set aside.

3 Generously season the inside of chicken with salt, pepper, paprika, and rosemary until insides are completely covered in spices. Place lemon wedges inside chicken. Drizzle remaining olive oil over chicken and rub to coat evenly. Sprinkle skin with salt, pepper, paprika, and rosemary to liking.

4 Place garlic in center of baking dish (in the middle of the potato circle). Place chicken on top of garlic, breasts facing up. Bake for 45 minutes, checking occasionally to ensure skin is not over-browning. If skin is browning too quickly, tent loosely with foil and continue baking.

5 Remove from oven. Using a large, flat spatula, tilt chicken to allow juices from inside to run into dish. Ladle juices from bottom of dish all over skin. Stir potatoes. Return chicken and potatoes to oven and cook for 30 more minutes, tenting again if necessary.

6 Remove from oven and let stand at room temperature for 10 minutes before carving.

7 Once chicken and potatoes are plated, ladle juice from baking dish over them and serve.

TIP

Use leftovers to make my
Zesty Tortilla Soup.

ZESTY TORTILLA SOUP

If chicken soup is good for the soul, then my tortilla soup will have your soul dancing the tango. Comforting, but with pizzazz, this recipe combines traditional chicken soup elements with Latin flavors that up the tempo on taste. Plus, this dish can be made from leftovers remaining from my Lemon and Garlic Spiced Chicken recipe – it's a great way to economize on cooking effort, so you can relax with a margarita while the soup heats up (which is also good for the soul).

8 medium heirloom tomatoes (about 32 oz.), peeled and quartered (see "Encore" section for peeling instructions)

1 tbsp. lactose-free butter

½ tsp. granulated sugar

1 dried chipotle chili (optional)

8 tbsp. diced green chilies

1 tsp. smoked paprika

1 tsp. ground black pepper

¼ tsp. chili powder

1 cup cooked, shredded chicken (I like to use the leftover chicken from my Lemon and Garlic Spiced Chicken)

1 ripe avocado, diced

½ cup lactose-free Monterey Jack, grated

10 crumbled tortilla chips

1 to 2 tbsp. cilantro, chopped

1 lime, quartered

1 Place tomatoes in a large stockpot and simmer over medium to medium-high heat. Stir in butter and sugar and continue heating until liquid has gathered in pot and tomatoes easily fall apart, about 15 minutes.

2 Stir in chipotle chili, diced green chilies, paprika, black pepper, and chili powder. Stir shredded chicken into tomato stock. Turn heat to low, cover, and heat for 10 minutes.

3 Divide avocado and grated cheese among soup bowls and set aside.

4 When soup is heated through, remove chipotle chili from pot and discard. Ladle soup into bowls atop avocado and cheese. Top with crumbled tortilla chips and cilantro, and squeeze lime juice on top. Prepare for your tastebuds to dance.

SERVES 4 to 6
EFFORT Easy to make but requires some time for peeling tomatoes and shredding chicken
ACTIVE PREP 30 to 35 minutes
PAIRING My Glorious Guacamole and Prickly Pear Margaritas

Calories: 290; Total Fat (g): 17; Saturated Fat (g): 3; Cholesterol (mg): 39; Sodium (mg): 270; Potassium (mg): 680; Total Carbohydrate (g): 18; Fiber (g): 5; Sugar (g): 7; Protein (g): 17. Content per serving. Assumes 6 servings.

TIP
If you aren't using leftover chicken from my Lemon and Garlic Spiced Chicken recipe, you can use the meat from a rotisserie chicken.

SPICY SALMON PATTIES

S

When I was growing up, one of my mom's standbys for a quick and healthy dinner was salmon patties. I always enjoyed their crispy, full flavor and ate them with gusto. Now I enjoy my own twist on mom's recipe because it's so easy to make. This dish can be a healthy summertime alternative to hamburgers and a fantastic wintertime meal when served with creamy mashed potatoes. Whatever the season, salmon patties are a great way to eat salmon that does not disappoint!

1 heaping handful of gluten-free crackers, crumbled

½ tsp. ground black pepper

¼ tsp. salt

15 oz. canned wild Alaskan pink or red salmon

1 egg, lightly beaten in a medium-size bowl

Hot sauce

2 tsp. lactose-free butter

4 to 5 lemon wedges

SERVES 4 to 6
EFFORT Easy enough for a weeknight
ACTIVE PREP 10 to 15 minutes
PAIRING Sauvignon Blanc

1 Mix crumbled crackers, black pepper, and salt in a bowl and set aside.

2 Empty contents of salmon can, including most of the liquid, into bowl containing beaten egg. Mix together with fingers until evenly combined.

3 Add cracker crumbs and several dashes of hot sauce to salmon. Continue to combine until all ingredients are thoroughly mixed. Salmon should be adhesive enough to form small patties. If consistency is still runny, add additional crumbled crackers until mixture is firm enough to form patties.

4 Shape salmon into small patties about ¾ inch thick.

5 Heat a non-stick skillet over medium to medium-high heat. Add butter to pan. Once butter has melted, swirl to coat bottom and add patties to skillet. Cook for 4 to 5 minutes per side, or until golden brown on both sides and cooked through.

6 Serve immediately with lemon for drizzling juice on top.

TIP

I recommend using Van's Multigrain Crispy Whole Grain Baked Crackers for this recipe.

Calories: 150; Total Fat (g): 7; Saturated Fat (g): 2; Cholesterol (mg): 78; Sodium (mg): 210; Potassium (mg): 270; Total Carbohydrate (g): 5; Fiber (g): 1; Sugar (g): 1; Protein (g): 16. Content per serving. Assumes 6 servings.

MS. FIT BURGER

I love burgers but don't always love how I feel after eating them. Seeking the juicy flavor of a burger without the "blahs," I created this veggie burger that is both delicious and healthy. Inspired by a popular burger served at a cafe in the Short North area of Columbus, beets and rice give this burger the look and texture of a meat patty, while black beans provide protein and iron. This burger tastes so good that even devoted carnivores will admit my Ms. Fit Burgers are anything but "blah."

1 Combine mashed beans and beets in a large bowl. Set aside.

2 Place green pepper, chopped onion, and garlic in a food processor and finely chop. Once chopped, pour into mashed beans and beets and combine.

3 In a separate bowl, whisk together egg, black pepper, paprika, and salt. Combine with bean and green pepper mixture and stir. Then stir rice into mixture until sticky. Add half of the thinly sliced onions and gradually stir in oat flour (adding just enough to help mixture stick together). Use hands to form 4 tightly packed patties.

4 Heat butter in a large skillet over medium to medium-high heat. Cook burgers for 3 minutes per side, or until outsides are slightly browned.

5 While burgers cook, sauté remaining onion slices in pan alongside patties. If using cheese, place on top of burgers while cooking to melt (I tend to put the cheese on immediately after the patties have been cooked on one side and I've flipped them over to begin cooking on the other side).

6 When burgers are ready, place in buns and top with sautéed onions and condiments. Serve.

Calories: 240; Total Fat (g): 4; Saturated Fat (g): 1; Cholesterol (mg): 54; Sodium (mg): 320; Potassium (mg): 250; Total Carbohydrate (g): 38; Fiber (g): 7; Sugar (g): 5; Protein (g): 11. Content per serving, exclusive of burger buns. Assumes 4 servings.

15 oz. canned black beans, rinsed, drained and mashed

3 medium beets, cooked and mashed

½ green bell pepper, chopped

¼ red onion, chopped + ½ red onion, thinly sliced

2 to 3 garlic cloves, minced

1 egg, lightly beaten (for vegan prep, soak 1 tbsp. flax meal in 3 tbsp. water for 5 minutes)

1 tsp. ground black pepper

1 tsp. smoked paprika

¼ tsp. salt

¼ to ½ cup rice, cooked

1 to 2 tbsp. gluten-free oat flour

1 tbsp. lactose-free butter

4 gluten-free burger buns

SERVES 4
EFFORT Better to make on a weekend
ACTIVE PREP 25 to 30 minutes
PAIRING Omission IPA

For low-lactose prep, top with Manchego Añejo slices.

CRAB CAKES 'N FOOTBALL

Named after a line from one of my favorite movies, *Wedding Crashers*, this dish is particularly enjoyable while watching a game on the gridiron. But if football's not in season, don't fret. It also goes great with a backyard gathering of friends. Or the creamy taste of pan-fried crab cakes can be dressed up with fetching sides for a fancy dinner. However you decide to enjoy them, you can be sure people will try to crash your party to get their hands on these cakes, football season or not.

8 oz. wild-caught crabmeat

1 egg, lightly beaten

⅓ cup gluten-free breadcrumbs

2 tbsp. mayonnaise

1½ tbsp. chives, finely chopped

1½ tsp. Dijon mustard

Juice from ¼ lemon

⅛ tsp. garlic powder

⅛ tsp. hot sauce

1 tbsp. lactose-free butter

1 Mix together all ingredients except butter in a large bowl. Once mixed, form 4 flat patties.

2 Heat a large non-stick skillet over medium to medium-high heat. Add butter to skillet, swirling to coat. Place cakes in skillet. Cook each side for about 3 to 4 minutes or until golden brown.

3 Remove cakes from skillet and serve.

SERVES 4

EFFORT Easy enough to make any time of day, including halftime of the big game

ACTIVE PREP 10 to 15 minutes

PAIRING Sparkling wine such as Cava, Prosecco, or, of course, Champagne

TIP

I recommend using crushed Glutino Original Bagel Chips as breadcrumbs for this recipe.

Calories: 230; Total Fat (g): 13; Saturated Fat (g): 2; Cholesterol (mg): 109; Sodium (mg): 450; Potassium (mg): 230; Total Carbohydrate (g): 13; Fiber (g): 7; Sugar (g): 2; Protein (g): 14. Content per serving. Assumes 4 servings.

MICHELLE'S CARNE ASADA

There's no better way to attract the attention of neighbors, not to mention their dogs, than firing up steaks at dinnertime. This recipe will have them all begging to come over for a taste. Tenderized by lime juice and flavored with garlic, ginger, jalapeno, and spices, my carne asada bursts with exotic zest sure to have mouths watering in no time. For great accompaniment, whip up my Crispy Steak Fries. But be sure to have extras on hand for all your new best friends in the neighborhood.

1 In a medium bowl, whisk together sour cream, half and half, garlic, lime juice, ginger, jalapeño pepper, chili powder, coriander, cumin, salt, and paprika.

2 Place meat in a shallow glass dish that is just large enough for it to fit. Pour marinade in dish and work into meat with fingers. Cover with foil and refrigerate for at least 4 hours, up to overnight.

3 About 30 minutes before you're ready to cook the beef, remove meat from fridge, keeping it in marinade, and allow to sit at room temperature.

4 Preheat a cast iron skillet over medium-high heat for 5 to 10 minutes. When skillet is heated, coat with 1 to 2 tsp. canola oil. Sear steaks in skillet for 3 to 4 minutes per side, depending on how well you like your steaks cooked. The outsides of steaks should have sear marks.

5 Remove steaks from skillet and allow to rest at room temperature for 3 to 5 minutes before serving.

SERVES 4 to 6
EFFORT Easy enough to make any day of the week.
ACTIVE PREP 15 to 20 minutes
PAIRING My Moscow Mule or Melville Pinot Noir

Calories: 370; Total Fat (g): 21; Saturated Fat (g): 8; Cholesterol (mg): 102; Sodium (mg): 300; Potassium (mg): 460; Total Carbohydrate (g): 2; Fiber (g): 0; Sugar (g): 1; Protein (g): 41. Content per serving. Assumes 6 servings.

¼ cup lactose-free sour cream

2 tbsp. lactose-free half and half

6 garlic cloves, minced

2 tbsp. fresh-squeezed lime juice

1-inch ginger root, peeled and minced (about 1½ tbsp.)

½ jalapeño pepper, minced (about 2 tbsp.)

1 tsp. chili powder

½ tsp. coriander

½ tsp. cumin

½ tsp. sea salt

½ tsp. smoked paprika

2 lbs. skirt steak or flap steak, excess fat trimmed and outer membrane removed

1 to 2 tsp. canola oil

TIP

Steaks may be broiled or grilled instead of seared in skillet. Cook time is the same regardless. Be sure broiler or grill is very hot before cooking so steaks will sear.

PAD THAI

There has been debate in my household about what exactly "umami" is. My husband asked me one day how I would describe the flavor, and I couldn't come up with a great verbal description. So I created this recipe: "This is what umami tastes like." Unlike lots of dishes with that special umami quality, this recipe incorporates no MSG, and is great for an array of diet plans. There's no controversy that this Pad Thai with chicken is tasty, extremely savory, and fun to eat. That's how you debate!

1 Combine tamarind paste, palm sugar, fish sauce, and red pepper flakes in a small bowl and set aside.

2 In a large, deep skillet or wok, heat canola oil over medium-high heat. Sauté shallot and garlic until they begin to soften.

3 Drain noodles and add to skillet, continuing to sauté. Add tamarind paste mixture and stir. Taste noodles to check if they are soft and chewy. If still firm, add a little water and continue cooking until desired texture is achieved. Make sure juices in skillet are soaked up.

4 Make space in the bottom of the pan for eggs. Scramble eggs until almost cooked through and then stir into noodles. Stir in chicken, 1 cup of bean sprouts, scallions, and a dash of white pepper. Serve with red pepper flakes, ½ cup bean sprouts, and lime wedges.

2 tbsp. tamarind paste

2 tbsp. palm sugar

4 tsp. fish sauce

½ tsp. red pepper flakes

2 tbsp. canola oil

1 shallot, minced

3 garlic cloves, minced

16 oz. dry Pad Thai rice noodles, soaked according to package instructions

3 eggs, very lightly beaten

4 to 6 oz. boneless, skinless chicken breasts, thinly sliced and cooked

1 cup bean sprouts for cooking + ½ cup as extra topping

3 scallions, chopped

Ground white pepper

1 lime, quartered

TIP

If you like peanuts in your Pad Thai, toast 2 tbsp. chopped peanuts in a skillet or wok. Serve as a topping alongside Pad Thai.

For vegetarian prep, omit chicken and fish sauce.

Calories: 320; Total Fat (g): 7; Saturated Fat (g): 1; Cholesterol (mg): 93; Sodium (mg): 300; Potassium (mg): 100; Total Carbohydrate (g): 53; Fiber (g): 1; Sugar (g): 4; Protein (g): 12. Content per serving. Assumes 8 servings.

SERVES 6 to 8
EFFORT Easy enough to make any day of the week
ACTIVE PREP 20 to 25 minutes
PAIRING Malbec

SHRIMP ON THE BARBIE

Whenever I visit my parents during the summer in Columbus, Ohio, my dad makes kebabs on the grill while we all sip iced tea and relax in the backyard. There's nothing quite like a lazy summertime evening with kebabs served over rice. Although my dad's kebabs usually are made with beef (and are delicious), I've found shrimp give this family favorite a light and healthy twist. So throw some shrimp on the barbie, sit back, and act like you're Down Under, even if you're really in the Midwest.

SKEWERS

1 lb. wild-caught jumbo shrimp (frozen or fresh, thawed if frozen)

2 large, firm tomatoes, quartered

2 medium red onions, quartered

2 green peppers cut into 1½-inch chunks

10 to 12 bamboo skewers, soaked in water for 30 minutes

1 to 2 cups dry rice, prepared according to package instructions

MARINADE

½ cup extra virgin olive oil

⅛ cup lemon juice

3 garlic cloves, minced

1½ tsp. salt

1½ tsp. granulated sugar

¼ tsp. ground black pepper

SERVES 4 to 6

EFFORT Suitable for a weeknight if shrimp are marinated the day before

ACTIVE PREP 30 to 35 minutes

PAIRING Iced tea or a white wine such as Clean Slate Riesling

1 At least 4 hours before serving, place shrimp in a single layer in a small, wide dish and set aside. Place vegetables in a separate large dish and set aside.

2 In a small bowl, vigorously mix marinade ingredients. Pour marinade over shrimp, coating generously and evenly. Add remainder of mixture to vegetables and toss. Cover each container with foil and refrigerate for 4 to 8 hours.

3 Once shrimp and vegetables have marinated, preheat broiler to high or set grill to medium-high heat. While broiler or grill heats, skewer shrimp and vegetables on separate skewers.

4 Place vegetable skewers on broiler or grill first since they will need to cook longer than shrimp, about 20 minutes total. Rotate vegetable skewers halfway through cooking time and cook until onions and peppers are slightly charred and tomatoes almost fall off of the skewers.

5 When 6 to 8 minutes are left for the vegetables, place the shrimp skewers on the broiler or grill, cooking 3 to 4 minutes per side. When shrimp are opaque and curling into a "c" shape, they're ready to be served. Serve shrimp and veggies over rice and sprinkle with seasoning mix (see Tip), if desired.

Calories: 300; Total Fat (g): 5; Saturated Fat (g): 1; Cholesterol (mg): 147; Sodium (mg): 250; Potassium (mg): 390; Total Carbohydrate (g): 41; Fiber (g): 2; Sugar (g): 5; Protein (g): 20. Content per serving, exclusive of rice. Assumes 6 servings.

TIP
A seasoning mix comprised of equal parts smoked paprika, garlic powder, chili powder, salt, and pepper can be sprinkled atop finished kebabs for added flavor.

Omit sugar and rice for paleo prep.

SIMPLE PORK TAMALES WITH CHIPOTLE SAUCE

Creamy, savory, and satisfying, tamales are fun-to-eat meals. Unfortunately, they also can be not-so-fun to make. Bringing masa harina dough to just the right texture and folding everything inside cornhusks can upset even the most jovial chefs. My recipe fixes these problems by using polenta in place of masa harina and omitting cornhusks. Turning tamales inside-out, this recipe will have your taste buds doing somersaults all while restoring balance to the eat/make fun equation.

PORK TAMALES

1 tbsp. garlic powder

½ tbsp. chili powder

½ tbsp. onion powder

½ tsp. ground black pepper

¼ tsp. sea salt

1 lb. boneless pork butt or shoulder

1 cup dry polenta, prepared according to package instructions

1 tsp. lactose-free butter

CHIPOTLE SAUCE

1 chipotle chili in adobo sauce, chopped + 2 tbsp. adobo sauce

½ cup lactose-free sour cream

1 Mix garlic powder, chili powder, onion powder, pepper, and salt in a small bowl. Rub mixture evenly over pork to coat. Cover and refrigerate for at least 4 hours and up to overnight.

2 Combine chipotle sauce ingredients in a small bowl. Cover and refrigerate until ready to serve.

3 Press polenta into an 8-by-8-inch glass baking dish, lightly greased with 1 tsp. butter. Cover and refrigerate.

4 Cook pork in slow cooker on low heat for 10 hours. Remove pork from slow cooker. Reserve juice and skim any fat off of the top. Shred pork with forks and return to slow cooker with skimmed juice, cooking for 30 minutes on low heat setting.

5 When ready to serve, slice polenta into 4 squares and warm in microwave. Top each square first with a touch of butter and then with warm pork. Spread chipotle sauce on top of pork with a knife. Serve immediately with extra chipotle sauce on the side.

SERVES 4 to 6

EFFORT Very easy. Just be sure to allot time for marinating and slow-cooking.

ACTIVE PREP 15 to 20 minutes

PAIRING My Electric Strawberry Lemonade

Tamales: Calories: 230; Total Fat (g): 10; Saturated Fat (g): 4; Cholesterol (mg): 47; Sodium (mg): 130; Potassium (mg): 240; Total Carbohydrate (g): 19; Fiber (g): 1; Sugar (g): 0; Protein (g): 15. Content per serving. Assumes 6 servings.

Sauce: Calories: 70; Total Fat (g): 7; Saturated Fat (g): 5; Cholesterol (mg): 23; Sodium (mg): 70; Potassium (mg): 0; Total Carbohydrate (g): 1; Fiber (g): 0; Sugar (g): 1; Protein (g): 1. Content per serving. Assumes 6 servings.

SALMON CURRY

I call it the Synergistic Property of Food Addition. This highly mathematical principle doesn't occur across all foods I love, but it arises enough to warrant its own name and scientific formula, which looks like this: Food I Love + Food I Love = Fantastic Food I Really Love. Well, the Property is most statistically significant in this dish, which melds my favorite fish with creamy, spicy red curry. Synergize with me and enjoy this curry when your taste buds need a Fantastic Food to Really Love.

15 oz. low fat coconut milk

2½ tbsp. red curry paste

1 tbsp. brown sugar or palm sugar

1 lb. wild-caught salmon fillet (thawed if frozen), cut into 1-inch cubes with gray meat removed

1 cup green beans (frozen or fresh)

½ yellow onion, thinly sliced

1 to 2 tsp. fish sauce

½ tsp. coriander

¼ tsp. cumin

2 cups dry jasmine rice, prepared according to package instructions

4 to 5 basil leaves, julienned

1 lime, quartered

1 Pour coconut milk into a large, deep skillet and heat over medium to medium-high heat until milk begins to simmer. When milk is simmering, stir in curry paste and brown/palm sugar. Allow mixture to heat for 3 to 5 minutes or until milk comes to a boil. Reduce heat to simmer.

2 Stir in salmon, green beans, and onion. Stir dish occasionally while simmering until salmon is cooked through but still moist, about 10 to 15 minutes. When salmon is cooked, turn off heat and stir in fish sauce, coriander, and cumin.

3 Ladle curry over rice, sprinkle basil leaves on top, and squeeze juice from lime over curry. Serve immediately.

SERVES 4 to 6
EFFORT So easy it can be made just about any day of the week
ACTIVE PREP 20 to 25 minutes
PAIRING Graves Blanc from Bordeaux or a Torrontes from Argentina

Calories: 300; Total Fat (g): 21; Saturated Fat (g): 15; Cholesterol (mg): 48; Sodium (mg): 350; Potassium (mg): 580; Total Carbohydrate (g): 9; Fiber (g): 2; Sugar (g): 4; Protein (g): 21. Content per serving, exclusive of rice. Assumes 6 servings.

BLACKENED MAHI-MAHI TACOS

The quintessential Baja fish taco is light-battered fish wrapped in corn tortilla and adorned with cabbage and mayo-based sauce. It can be great, but the frying often weighs it down. Baked or grilled fish can replace the fried fillet, though something, like flavor, seems to get lost in translation. This recipe nixes batter and eschews bland, so you'll never go back to floured fillets or tasteless tacos. Plus, this recipe is so versatile that it can be made with langostinos, tilapia, or halibut. Go fish!

1 Mix dry rub ingredients together in a small bowl. Rub mixture over mahi-mahi fillets, coating evenly and thoroughly.

2 Heat butter in a cast iron skillet over medium-high heat. Once butter has melted, place fillets in skillet and cook for 3 to 4 minutes per side, or until blackened and firm.

3 While fillets cook, mix sour cream and salsa in a small bowl. Set aside.

4 Just before fish is finished cooking, warm tortillas in a skillet over medium heat until they are pliable, about 30 to 60 seconds. I recommend coating the skillet with ½ tsp. butter before adding tortillas to prevent sticking.

5 When mahi-mahi is ready, divide among tortillas. Top with shredded cabbage, radish, and sour cream/salsa mixture. Add a squeeze of lime and serve.

DRY RUB

2 tbsp. garlic powder

1 tbsp. dried oregano

1 tbsp. dried thyme

1 tbsp. chili powder

1 tbsp. ground black pepper

2½ tsp. smoked paprika

1 tsp. sea salt

TACOS

1 lb. wild-caught mahi-mahi fillets (frozen, thawed fillets work great)

2 tbsp. lactose-free butter

2 tbsp. lactose-free sour cream

1 tbsp. tomato-based salsa

4 to 8 soft corn tortilla shells

Shredded cabbage

1 radish, sliced into very thin rounds

1 lime, quartered

Calories: 290; Total Fat (g): 11; Saturated Fat (g): 3; Cholesterol (mg): 115; Sodium (mg): 630; Potassium (mg): 680; Total Carbohydrate (g): 20; Fiber (g): 2; Sugar (g): 1; Protein (g): 29. Content per serving. Assumes 4 servings.

SERVES 2 to 4
EFFORT Simple enough for a weeknight
ACTIVE PREP 15 to 20 minutes
PAIRING Omission Lager

HOMESTEAD QUINOA CHILI

This dish is based on my parents' hearty Midwestern chili recipe, which is the perfect food to warm up a shivery autumn evening. I've substituted red quinoa for their recipe's ground beef and added a few seasonings that up the warmth even more and round out the chili's flavor. While canned tomatoes can be substituted for the heirlooms, I prefer to use fresh ones, which provide a clean taste and eliminate any bisphenol-A (BPA) that can be present in the canned variety.

2 tbsp. extra virgin olive oil

3 green bell peppers, diced

2 yellow onions, diced

3 garlic cloves, minced

4 giant (about 5 inches across) heirloom tomatoes, peeled and quartered (see "Encore" section for peeling instructions)

2 cups red quinoa, rinsed

30 oz. canned red kidney beans, rinsed

2 heaping tbsp. chili powder

1 tsp. smoked paprika

½ to 1 tsp. cayenne pepper

1 tsp. cumin

½ tsp. coriander

½ tsp. ground black pepper

¼ tsp. salt

¼ tsp. cinnamon

⅓ oz. dark chocolate

1 Heat olive oil over medium-low heat in a large, deep pot. Add peppers, onions, and garlic. Sauté until soft, about 5 minutes.

2 Add tomatoes, quinoa, beans, spices, and chocolate to pot and mix thoroughly. Turn heat to high and continue stirring until liquid boils. Once liquid reaches boil, reduce heat and cover. Simmer until quinoa has absorbed most of the liquid, about 25 minutes, stirring occasionally. Serve.

SERVES 6 to 8
EFFORT Great to make Sunday afternoon and eat all week
ACTIVE PREP 35 to 40 minutes
PAIRING Spanish Tempranillo like Viña Cubillo Crianza from Rioja, or Green's Gluten Free Endeavor Dubbel Dark Ale

TIP

For Paleo preparation, substitute 3 pounds of ground beef for quinoa and omit beans and chocolate. Brown beef with peppers, onions, and garlic. Simmer for 1 hour.

Calories: 390; Total Fat (g): 13; Saturated Fat (g): 3; Cholesterol (mg): 0; Sodium (mg): 340; Potassium (mg): 700; Total Carbohydrate (g): 61; Fiber (g): 11; Sugar (g): 15; Protein (g): 13. Content per serving. Assumes 8 servings.

CHICKEN FAJITA QUESADILLAS

While in college, I frequented a Mexican restaurant in town more than I'd like to admit. The place was college budget friendly, and its fajita quesadillas – sautéed onions and peppers, seasoned chicken, and fresh tortillas – were irresistible. I couldn't get enough of them. Fast-forward to today. My college years are well past, and fajita quesadillas are off limits due to gluten and lactose sensitivities. This recipe satifies pangs for comida Mexicana (*sin gluten o queso con lactosa*).

DRY RUB

2 tsp. smoked paprika

1 tsp. chili powder

½ tsp. cumin

½ tsp. onion powder

½ tsp. garlic powder

½ tsp. ground black pepper

¼ tsp. or less salt

QUESADILLAS

1 lb. free-range chicken breast tenders or wild-caught shrimp, peeled and deveined

2 tsp. canola oil

1 yellow onion, thinly sliced

1 green bell pepper, thinly sliced

4 rice flour tortillas

4 oz. lactose-free Monterey Jack, grated

SERVES 4 to 6
EFFORT Easy enough to make on a busy weeknight
ACTIVE PREP 20 to 25 minutes
PAIRING My Southwest Salsa or my Glorious Guacamole

1 In a small bowl, mix together dry rub ingredients. Rub seasoning all over chicken tenders or shrimp to coat. Set aside.

2 In a large cast iron or non-stick skillet, heat canola oil over medium-high heat. Once oil is heated, sauté onion, pepper, and chicken in skillet, stirring frequently. Cook until chicken is cooked through and vegetables are soft, about 7 to 10 minutes. If using shrimp, sauté vegetables for 3 to 5 minutes before adding shrimp to the skillet. Cook shrimp for 1 to 2 minutes per side with vegetables.

3 Place each tortilla on a plate and top with Monterey Jack. Microwave each tortilla on high for 20 to 25 seconds or until cheese is melted.

4 Transfer meat and vegetables to tortillas using a slotted spoon. Fold tortilla over contents. Serve.

 For vegetarian/vegan prep, substitute 10 oz. mushrooms. Use Follow Your Heart Vegan Gourmet Monterey Jack.

Calories: 310; Total Fat (g): 14; Saturated Fat (g): 2; Cholesterol (mg): 64; Sodium (mg): 340; Potassium (mg): 260; Total Carbohydrate (g): 21; Fiber (g): 4; Sugar (g): 2; Protein (g): 25. Content per serving, using chicken. Assumes 6 servings.

Tuna melts have been a lunchtime standby in my household for years because they're such an easy way to incorporate fish into the diet. Of course, with bread and cheese as key ingredients in traditional tuna melts, I had to reinvent things a bit to accommodate our dietary needs. The reinvention led to good things: In addition to banning gluten and lactose, I invited Dijon mustard and bell pepper to the party. Chicken of the sea? More like lord of the lunch table.

1 Preheat oven to 400 degrees.

2 Scoop tuna into a small bowl and break meat apart with a fork. Add diced bell pepper, mayonnaise, mustard, lemon juice, and hot sauce (if using) to bowl. Mix.

3 Divide meat in half, placing each half on top of a slice of bread and pressing meat down with the flat side of the fork, forming a patty atop bread. Place second piece of bread on top.

4 In a large skillet, heat olive oil over medium to medium-high heat. Place tuna sandwiches in skillet and cook for 2 minutes on each side or until outsides of bread are lightly browned. Remove sandwiches from skillet and place on a foil baking tray.

5 Remove top from each sandwich and sprinkle cheddar on top of meat. Heat in oven until cheese has melted, about 5 to 10 minutes. Remove sandwiches from oven, replace top bread slice, and serve.

5 oz. canned tuna in water, drained
¼ red or green bell pepper, diced
1 to 1½ tbsp. mayonnaise
2 tsp. Dijon mustard
Juice from ½ lemon
Dash of hot sauce (optional)
4 slices gluten-free bread
1 to 2 tsp. extra virgin olive oil
Lactose-free shredded cheddar

SERVES 2 to 3
EFFORT Easy enough to make any day of the week
ACTIVE PREP 15 to 20 minutes.
PAIRING Lemonade or iced tea

TIP
For low-lactose preparation, I recommend Trader Joe's X-tra X-tra Sharp New York Cheddar Cheese.

Calories: 280; Total Fat (g): 10; Saturated Fat (g): 1; Cholesterol (mg): 10; Sodium (mg): 430; Potassium (mg): 110; Total Carbohydrate (g): 28; Fiber (g): 2; Sugar (g): 3; Protein (g): 15. Content per serving. Assumes 3 servings.

TP

If you want to cut down on prep time, try topping chops with unsweetened apple-sauce and omit spiced apple prepara-tion.

POSH SPICED PORK CHOPS

Nothing says luxurious comfort food like pan-seared pork chops served atop a bed of mashed potatoes. When garnished with spiced apples, this dish warms the soul, nourishes the body, and provides lasting sweetness on the palate. This recipe is at its best when the pork chops have been brined to tenderize the meat and when apples are in season. For classy comfort at its finest, I recommend pairing this dish with a glowing fire and good company. That's what I call posh spice.

1 Bring 1 cup water to a boil in a small saucepan. Once water is boiling, stir in ½ tbsp. salt, ½ tsp. pepper, and garlic. Add 2 cups cold water to saucepan.

2 Place pork chops in a shallow dish. When brine has reached room temperature, pour over chops. Cover and refrigerate for 30 minutes to 4 hours.

3 Melt butter in a large skillet over medium heat. Add brown sugar and stir for about 2 minutes. Add apples to skillet and cook until they are slightly softened, about 2 minutes. Then add onion and cook for another 5 minutes, stirring occasionally.

4 Add ½ tsp. pepper, orange juice, cider vinegar, honey, cinnamon, and a dash of salt to skillet. Continue cooking mixture over medium heat, stirring occasionally, until the liquid thickens, about 5 minutes. Remove from heat and set aside.

5 Preheat oven to 400 degrees. Heat a cast iron skillet over medium-high heat.

6 Remove chops from brine and pat dry. Lightly coat outsides with olive oil and season with salt and pepper.

7 Sear chops in pan, about 3 to 4 minutes per side. Flip chops and place skillet in oven. Bake until pork is cooked through, 15 to 20 minutes for thick cuts and 5 to 10 minutes for thinner chops.

8 Place chops in a dish and cover loosely with foil. Pour skillet juice over the chops. Allow to rest at room temperature for about 5 minutes. Top with apple mixture and serve.

3 cups water

½ tbsp. salt for brine + additional salt for seasoning chops

1 tsp. ground black pepper + additional pepper for seasoning chops

2 garlic cloves, crushed

4 bone-in pork chops

2 tbsp. lactose-free butter

2 tbsp. brown sugar

2 Granny Smith apples, peeled, cored, and cut into ¼-inch thick slices

1 yellow onion, thinly sliced

⅛ cup orange juice

1 tsp. cider vinegar

1 tsp. honey

¼ tsp. cinnamon

Extra virgin olive oil

SERVES 6 to 8
EFFORT This dish is straightforward but time-consuming
ACTIVE PREP 45 minutes
PAIRING Epiphany Grenache Blanc

Calories: 330; Total Fat (g): 19; Saturated Fat (g): 6; Cholesterol (mg): 86; Sodium (mg): 770; Potassium (mg): 430; Total Carbohydrate (g): 12; Fiber (g): 1; Sugar (g): 10; Protein (g): 26. Content per serving. Assumes 8 servings.

HOMEMADE SPAGHETTI MEAT SAUCE

Running is one of my favorite hobbies, which is a good thing since another of my hobbies is eating. I've found the two are never more compatible than when I pair spaghetti dinner with a long run the next morning. Great fuel for cardio and a consistent performer when picky eaters arrive as guests, my spaghetti sauce is crisp, low in sodium, and BPA-free. Deliberately unfussy, this is a tasty, healthy winner that's perfect whether you're fueling up for a run or running a dinner party for finicky guests.

2 tsp. lactose-free butter

5 to 6 ripe heirloom tomatoes, peeled and chopped (see "Encore" section for peeling instructions)

¼ tsp. granulated sugar

1 tbsp. extra virgin olive oil

½ yellow onion, diced

½ red bell pepper, diced

4 oz. mushrooms, sliced

2 garlic cloves, minced

½ lb. 85% lean grass-fed ground beef

½ tsp. ground black pepper

½ tsp. smoked paprika

¼ tsp. sea salt

Crushed red pepper flakes

8 oz. dry gluten-free spaghetti, prepared according to package instructions

Fresh basil leaves, julienned

Lactose-free Parmesan or Aged Parmesan cheese, grated (optional)

1 Heat butter in a large saucepan over medium heat and add tomatoes and sugar. Cook until tomatoes break apart, about 15 minutes. Set aside.

2 In a large, deep skillet, heat olive oil over medium-high heat. Sauté onion, bell pepper, mushroom, and garlic. Cook until onion is translucent and mushrooms are cooked down, about 5 to 10 minutes.

3 Stir ground beef into skillet and continue sautéing until meat is cooked through but not tough, about 7 to 10 minutes.

4 Pour meat mixture from skillet into saucepan containing tomatoes. Stir in pepper, paprika, salt, and red pepper flakes. Bring sauce to a boil, then reduce heat to simmer, stirring occasionally. Allow sauce to simmer for 10 to 15 minutes.

5 Serve sauce over spaghetti noodles and top with basil leaves and Parmesan.

TIP

I recommend asking your butcher to grind fresh beef (or grind it yourself).

SERVES 2 to 4
EFFORT Practice a few times before making on a weeknight
ACTIVE PREP 40 to 45 minutes
PAIRING Chianti Classico

Calories: 430; Total Fat (g): 17; Saturated Fat (g): 3; Cholesterol (mg): 34; Sodium (mg): 200; Potassium (mg): 700; Total Carbohydrate (g): 57; Fiber (g): 4; Sugar (g): 9; Protein (g): 16. Content per serving. Assumes 4 servings.

SARDINE AND TOMATO TOSTA

With all the unavoidable complexity in the world these days, there's something to be said for simplicity. This recipe, inspired by the essential flavors of Spanish food, revels in simplicity without forgoing flavor or sacrificing salubrity. Perfect for lunchtime, sardines and tomatoes on gluten-free toast provide an outsize helping of omega-3 fatty acids in an easy-to-enjoy format that will have you looking forward to lunch and loving your afternoons. If only everything were this simple!

1 medium red, flavorful tomato (ideally heirloom or organic), sliced

Extra virgin olive oil

2 to 3 slices gluten-free bread, toasted to liking

Salt

Ground black pepper

Smoked paprika

1 tin sardines in olive oil, about 3.5 oz., drained

1 Heat a small, non-stick skillet over medium heat. Add tomato slices and heat until warm, about 2 minutes per side.

2 Drizzle olive oil over toast, top with tomato slices and season to taste with salt, pepper, and paprika. Top with sardines and serve immediately.

SERVES 2
EFFORT Easy enough for a rushed day
ACTIVE PREP 10 minutes
PAIRING Daura Damm

TIP

Anchovy fillets may be used in place of sardines, just be mindful of anchovies' sodium.

Calories: 240; Total Fat (g): 9; Saturated Fat (g): 0; Cholesterol (mg): 70; Sodium (mg): 330; Potassium (mg): 340; Total Carbohydrate (g): 23; Fiber (g): 2; Sugar (g): 5; Protein (g): 15. Content per serving. Assumes 2 servings.

SAMBA CHICKEN AND PLANTAINS

When I'm in the mood for chicken but feel like changing the flavors' rhythms a bit, this is the recipe I reach for. Each element of this dish can be spun together with relative ease, and the flavors dance a sweet and savory two-step to perfection. Serve alongside rice and beans for a balanced and tasty combination of carbs and amino acids. With my salsa to spice things up, this recipe is one that will have you dancing the samba!

1 Preheat oven to 450 degrees. Line a baking sheet with foil and lightly coat with cooking spray.

2 Arrange plantains in single layer on baking sheet and coat tops with cooking spray. Bake for 7 minutes. Remove from oven, flip plantains, and top with a little butter, brown sugar, and cinnamon. Continue baking for 8 minutes or until plantains are lightly browned on the outside.

3 In a small bowl, mix dry spices for chicken. Sprinkle mixture on chicken tenders and rub in to coat.

4 Heat olive oil in a non-stick skillet over medium-high heat. Place chicken tenders in skillet and cook until browned and heated through, about 4 to 5 minutes per side.

5 While chicken cooks, combine salsa ingredients in a small bowl and stir.

6 When ready, top chicken with salsa and serve alongside plantains.

SERVES 4 to 6
EFFORT Easier than it looks but better to make on a weekend
ACTIVE PREP 30 to 35 minutes
PAIRING My Moscow Mule

Calories: 380; Total Fat (g): 9; Saturated Fat (g): 2; Cholesterol (mg): 63; Sodium (mg): 140; Potassium (mg): 550; Total Carbohydrate (g): 49; Fiber (g): 2; Sugar (g): 13; Protein (g): 25. Content per serving, exclusive of salsa. Assumes 6 servings.

PLANTAINS*

Cooking spray
1 to 2 ripe plantains, peeled and sliced diagonally into ½-inch thick rounds
1 to 2 tsp. lactose-free butter
Brown sugar or palm sugar
Cinnamon (optional)

CHICKEN

1 tsp. oregano
1 tsp. cumin
½ tsp. ground black pepper
¼ tsp. salt
1 lb. free-range chicken breast tenders
2 tsp. extra virgin olive oil

SALSA

1 cup frozen mango cubes, thawed and chopped into ¼-inch cubes
¼ cup fresh-squeezed lime juice
1 garlic clove, minced
½ to 1 tbsp. finely chopped cilantro leaves
½ tsp. honey
¼ tsp. each smoked paprika, cumin, and allspice

*Omit for Paleo prep.

SALADS & SIDES

While I love the way I feel when I eat my veggies, I admittedly don't always love their flavor. My salads and sides recipes take the most challenging superfoods, like kale and broccoli, and turn them into delights that will satisfy even the pickiest palates.

Flavorful and packed with vitamins and antioxidants, these recipes are the perfect way to incorporate a few servings of vegetables into your diet and are just about as much fun to eat as any main course. They're so good, in fact, that meat-lovers had better beware: Once you've tried these veggies, you might never crave ribeyes or roasts again. Well, almost never.

WATERMELON AND QUINOA SALAD

This recipe was inspired by a salad I had while vacationing in Santa Barbara. Nearing the end of my trip, I was looking for a healthy lunch on a sunny afternoon, so when I saw watermelon and quinoa salad on a restaurant menu, I was sold. My meal was so refreshing that I had to create my very own version. This is it – flavorful and invigorating enough to evoke the sun and surf of Santa Barbara every time it's eaten. The trick to a great rendition of this salad is finding a ripe, sweet watermelon.

SALAD

7 oz. arugula

½ red pepper, julienned

½ cucumber, sliced into small quarters

½ cup shredded carrots

A handful each of dried cranberries, chopped walnuts, and crumbled lactose-free feta-style cheese

1 cup dry red quinoa, prepared according to package instructions and chilled

1 small watermelon, sliced into spears

Balsamic glaze

DRESSING

¼ cup extra virgin olive oil

2 tbsp. fresh-squeezed lemon juice

1 tbsp. balsamic vinegar

1 garlic clove, minced

½ tsp. agave syrup

¼ tsp. ground black pepper

⅛ tsp. salt

1 Vigorously whisk dressing ingredients together in a small bowl or shake in a tightly sealed glass jar.

2 Place arugula, red pepper, cucumber, and carrots in a large mixing bowl. Toss with dressing. Divide salad among serving bowls and sprinkle with cranberries and walnuts.

3 Place one heaping spoonful of quinoa on each salad and top with watermelon spears and crumbled cheese (use vegan cheese for vegan prep). Drizzle with balsamic glaze and season with salt and pepper to taste. Serve.

....

SERVES 4
EFFORT If quinoa is premade, this salad can be whipped together anytime
ACTIVE PREP 15 to 20 minutes
PAIRING Sparkling water or my Balsamic Spritzer

Salad: Calories: 310; Total Fat (g): 10; Saturated Fat (g): 1; Cholesterol (mg): 0; Sodium (mg): 50; Potassium (mg): 410; Total Carbohydrate (g): 50; Fiber (g): 6; Sugar (g): 16; Protein (g): 10. Content per serving. Assumes 4 servings.

Dressing: Calories: 130; Total Fat (g): 14; Saturated Fat (g): 2; Cholesterol (mg): 0; Sodium (mg): 60; Potassium (mg): 10; Total Carbohydrate (g): 2; Fiber (g): 0; Sugar (g): 1; Protein (g): 0. Content per serving. Assumes 4 servings.

TIP

A ripe watermelon will have a big yellow sunspot and light brown lines called "bee stings." It should feel heavy for its size and make a deep sound if you knock on it. For vegan prep, use nut milk cheese.

SNEAKY GREEK SALAD

This recipe is named after its dressing, which (sneakily) incorporates anchovies in way that could go undetected even by those who swear they'd never eat them. In fact, I've found it's those same stubborn eaters who most love the tangy flavor. With tomatoes, cucumber, olives, red onion, and crumbled lactose-free cheese, this dish has all the elements of a great Greek salad, plus gluten-free croutons. It hits the spot on a warm summer day. Pop open some Greek wine and say *Opa!*

SALAD

2 slices gluten-free bread, toasted

1 to 2 tsp. lactose-free butter

1 garlic clove, minced

3 hearts romaine lettuce, chopped into bite-size leaves

1 small to medium tomato, diced

½ cucumber, sliced into ¼-inch thick rounds

½ bell pepper, julienned

½ cup kalamata olives

¼ red onion, thinly sliced

¼ cup lactose-free feta-style cheese, crumbled

DRESSING

¼ cup fresh-squeezed lemon juice

2 garlic cloves minced

1 to 2 anchovy fillets, rinsed and dried

1 tsp. dried basil leaves

1 tsp. ground black pepper

½ to 1 tsp. granulated sugar

¼ tsp. sea salt

¼ cup extra virgin olive oil

1 To make dressing, place all dressing ingredients except olive oil in a food processor and process until anchovy fillets are finely chopped. Slowly add olive oil and continue processing until ingredients are thoroughly mixed. Pour contents into re-sealable container and place in refrigerator. Shake vigorously just before serving.

2 Preheat oven to 375 degrees. Butter toasted bread and sprinkle with minced garlic. Bake garlic-buttered toast for 5 to 7 minutes on foil baking sheet.

3 Meanwhile, place remaining salad ingredients in a large bowl and toss with dressing. Divide among serving bowls.

4 Remove bread from oven and slice into croutons (about ¼-inch to ½-inch squares). Top salads with croutons and serve.

SERVES 4
EFFORT Easy if dressing is made in advance
ACTIVE PREP 15 to 20 minutes
PAIRING Iced tea or Greek white wine

Salad: Calories: 150; Total Fat (g): 8; Saturated Fat (g): 1; Cholesterol (mg): 0; Sodium (mg): 220; Potassium (mg): 260; Total Carbohydrate (g): 17; Fiber (g): 2; Sugar (g): 4; Protein (g): 3. Content per serving. Assumes 4 servings.

Dressing: Calories: 140; Total Fat (g): 14; Saturated Fat (g): 2; Cholesterol (mg): 2; Sodium (mg): 210; Potassium (mg): 30; Total Carbohydrate (g): 3; Fiber (g): 0; Sugar (g): 1; Protein (g): 1. Content per serving. Assumes 4 servings.

TIP

Top salad with marinated, grilled chicken or shrimp for a heartier, protein-packed meal. Italian dressing makes a great marinade. Just place meat in a glass baking dish, pour a generous amount of dressing over meat, cover, and refrigerate for at least 3 hours. Grill to liking.

RED THAI QUINOA AND KALE SALAD

Quinoa and kale have enjoyed a meteoric rise in popularity – and with good reason. Their health benefits are too numerous to list, they provide great flavor and texture, and they're incredibly versatile. So what happens when you put them together? An outta-this-world dining experience. Red coconut curry lends some celestial spice, while cabbage, carrots, red pepper, and onion form the rest of this constellation of flavors. Enjoy this stellar salad anytime you want to boost your day into higher orbit.

1 Prepare quinoa according to package instructions, using coconut milk in place of water. Stir in red curry paste and brown/palm sugar and continue cooking until liquid is absorbed.

2 Meanwhile, fill a large pot with water, add a dash of salt, and bring water to a boil. While water heats, fill another large bowl or pot with cold water and set aside.

3 When water reaches boil, insert kale and boil for 3 to 4 minutes. Remove kale from boiling water with slotted spoon and immediately place in cold water bath. Keep water in stovetop pot boiling for cabbage and carrots.

4 While kale cools, place cabbage and carrots in boiling water for 90 seconds. Drain water from pot and place drained carrots and cabbage in cold water bath with kale for 2 to 3 minutes. Remove vegetables from bath, dry, and place them in a large mixing bowl. When ready, add quinoa mixture and red peppers and onion to bowl. Toss to mix ingredients. Squeeze lime juice over salad and sprinkle with salt to taste. Serve.

1 cup dry red or white quinoa

14 oz. low-fat coconut milk

2 tbsp. red curry paste

½ tbsp. brown sugar or palm sugar

10 oz. chopped kale, stems removed

1 cup shredded cabbage

1 cup shredded carrots

½ red bell pepper, diced and sautéed

½ yellow onion, diced and sautéed

1 lime, quartered

Salt

SERVES 4
EFFORT This dish is not difficult to make, but it requires some time
ACTIVE PREP 30 to 35 minutes
PAIRING Torrontes from Argentina or a Fess Parker Pinot Noir

TIP Add some toasted cashews to this salad to give it a bit more heft.

Calories: 310; Total Fat (g): 8; Saturated Fat (g): 4; Cholesterol (mg): 0; Sodium (mg): 260; Potassium (mg): 520; Total Carbohydrate (g): 53; Fiber (g): 8; Sugar (g): 11; Protein (g): 11. Content per serving. Assumes 4 servings.

It's been said the taco salad pioneered the art of making salads unhealthy. Well, so much for that. This taco salad provides balanced and tasty nutrition, with plenty of vegetables, beans, and grass-fed beef, all topped by zesty cilantro-lime dressing. For a finishing touch, spiced and baked rice flour tortilla strips add great crunch. With so many wholesome ingredients and so much flavor, there isn't any room for unhealthy in this taco salad. A dish with the taste of tacos and the virtue of veggies – now, that's what I call art.

SERVES 4 to 6
EFFORT Takes some work
ACTIVE PREP 35 to 40 minutes
PAIRING Limeade or my Electric Strawberry Lemonade

Salad: Calories: 340; Total Fat (g): 17; Saturated Fat (g): 3; Cholesterol (mg): 45; Sodium (mg): 270; Potassium (mg): 540; Total Carbohydrate (g): 28; Fiber (g): 8; Sugar (g): 2; Protein (g): 20. Content per serving. Assumes 6 servings.

Dressing: Calories: 90; Total Fat (g): 9; Saturated Fat (g): 1; Cholesterol (mg): 0; Sodium (mg): 80; Potassium (mg): 20; Total Carbohydrate (g): 1; Fiber (g): 0; Sugar (g): 0; Protein (g): 0. Content per serving. Assumes 6 servings.

HEALTHY TACO SALAD

1 Preheat oven to 350 degrees.

2 Mix taco seasoning ingredients in a small bowl and set aside.

3 Line baking sheet with foil and place tortilla strips on baking sheet. Spray lightly with cooking oil and sprinkle with a dash of taco seasoning. Bake until strips are crispy, about 5 to 7 minutes.

4 While tortillas bake, place lettuce, black beans, corn, avocado, bell pepper, onion, and carrots in a large salad bowl, cover, and refrigerate.

5 Heat a large skillet over medium heat. Add beef. Stir in taco seasoning and ¼ cup water. Sauté until beef is cooked through, about 7 to 10 minutes. When beef is ready, remove skillet from heat and set aside.

6 In a blender or food processor, mix dressing ingredients on low speed until thoroughly mixed. Dressing should have small cilantro chunks.

7 Remove salad from refrigerator. Toss with dressing and divide among serving bowls. Using a slotted spoon, place meat on top of salads. Top with tortilla strips and cheddar. Serve.

TIP

For vegetarian preparation, use quinoa in place of beef. Prepare quinoa according to package instructions and stir in taco seasoning while cooking. For vegan prep, use quinoa and Daiya Cheddar Shreds.

SALAD

1 rice flour tortilla, sliced into 3-inch strips

3 Romaine lettuce hearts, chopped

15 oz. canned black beans, drained

1 ear of corn, kernels shaved

1 avocado, diced

1 red bell pepper, julienned

½ red onion, thinly sliced

½ cup shredded carrots

1 lb. grass-fed ground beef

¼ cup lactose-free shredded cheddar

TACO SEASONING

2 tsp. chili powder

2 tsp. smoked paprika

1 tsp. cumin

½ tsp. garlic powder

½ tsp. onion powder

½ tsp. ground black pepper

¼ to ½ tsp. salt

Dash of red pepper flakes

DRESSING

¼ cup extra virgin olive oil

¼ cup fresh-squeezed lime juice

2 garlic cloves

2 tbsp. cilantro leaves

½ tbsp. orange juice

¼ to ½ tsp. salt

Dash of coriander

¼ jalapeño pepper (optional)

TIP

This recipe makes a great meal on the go. Just store the salad contents and dressing in separate, tightly sealed containers and refrigerate. When ready to eat, pour dressing into salad container, reseal, and shake to combine.

KALE SALAD WITH LEMON VINAIGRETTE

Recognizing how healthy raw kale can be, I was determined to prepare it in a way my husband would agree to eat. I finally found it with this recipe. A bit like garlicky pasta, but with kale instead of noodles, this salad is packed with healthy goodies and zesty flavor. I feel great after I've eaten this for lunch and even my husband admits he enjoys this meal. One trick to making the dish palatable and easy to eat is removing the fibrous stems from kale leaves, which can be difficult to chew.

1 Vigorously whisk dressing ingredients together in a small bowl or shake in a tightly sealed glass jar.

2 Place kale and cabbage in a large salad bowl and toss with dressing until leaves are thoroughly coated.

3 Dish into serving bowls. Top with cheese, walnuts, and roasted garlic cloves (if using). Serve.

SALAD

10 oz. chopped kale, stems removed

1 cup shredded cabbage

2 generous handfuls of shaved Parmigiano-Reggiano or lactose-free Parmesan

2 handfuls of walnuts

1 head of garlic, roasted in the oven (optional; see "Encore" section for roasting instructions)

DRESSING

¼ cup extra virgin olive oil

¼ cup fresh-squeezed lemon juice

3 garlic cloves, minced

1 tsp. dried oregano

1 tsp. granulated sugar

½ tsp. ground black pepper

½ tsp. thyme

½ tsp. rosemary

⅛ tsp. salt

Salad: Calories: 160; Total Fat (g): 11; Saturated Fat (g): 2; Cholesterol (mg): 4; Sodium (mg): 110; Potassium (mg): 400; Total Carbohydrate (g): 12; Fiber (g): 2; Sugar (g): 1; Protein (g): 8. Content per serving. Assumes 4 servings.

Dressing: Calories: 130; Total Fat (g): 14; Saturated Fat (g): 2; Cholesterol (mg): 0; Sodium (mg): 70; Potassium (mg): 20; Total Carbohydrate (g): 3; Fiber (g): 0; Sugar (g): 1; Protein (g): 0. Content per serving. Assumes 4 servings.

SERVES 4

EFFORT Easy enough to make any day of the week

ACTIVE PREP 15 minutes

PAIRING Pizza

ROASTED BEET SALAD

Beets may have a bad rap in the flavor department, but when it comes to anti-inflammatory and cancer-fighting properties, they're hard to beat (pun unapologetically intended). This recipe is the perfect way to incorporate beets into your diet with a tasty preparation. Plus, it's so easy to make that it leaves no excuse for their absence in your meals. Did I mention that beets are also high in vitamins and antioxidants that fight free radicals and oxidative stress? So go on; just beet it.

1 Preheat oven to 400 degrees and line baking sheet with foil.

2 In a small bowl, whisk together garlic, olive oil, and vinegar. Stir in desired amounts of thyme, salt, and pepper.

3 Coat beets in balsamic vinaigrette, reserving some as dressing for salad. Place beets on baking sheet and bake for 15 minutes, or until they begin to brown.

4 Remove beets from oven and distribute among salad bowls. Top with cheese and pistachio nutmeats. Drizzle remaining balsamic dressing over salads and serve immediately.

SALAD

8 oz. baby beets, steamed or roasted, peeled, and quartered

2 tbsp. lactose-free feta-style cheese, crumbled

¼ cup pistachio nutmeats, dry roasted and unsalted

DRESSING

1 garlic clove, minced

2 tbsp. extra virgin olive oil

2 tbsp. balsamic vinegar

Thyme

Salt

Ground black pepper

SERVES 4
EFFORT Can easily be pulled together in minutes
ACTIVE PREP 5 to 10 minutes
PAIRING Grilled steaks

TIP Omit cheese for Paleo and vegan preparation. Or, for vegan, use nut milk cheese.

Calories: 130; Total Fat (g): 10; Saturated Fat (g): 2; Cholesterol (mg): 4; Sodium (mg): 40; Potassium (mg): 150; Total Carbohydrate (g): 10; Fiber (g): 1; Sugar (g): 6; Protein (g): 2. Assumes 4 servings.

GARLIC SESAME GREEN BEANS

As important as they are, it often seems vegetable sides are an afterthought. With so much attention and energy focused on the main event, it's difficult to have a lot of extra bandwidth for preparing complicated side dishes. Which leads to uninspired, steamed vegetables that fall short on flavor. This dish is one answer to the dilemma. Like many of my vegetable side recipes, this one is very simple to make and adds a great punch of taste to the greenest of greens.

1 lb. fresh green beans, stems removed

2 tsp. canola oil

3 garlic cloves, finely sliced

1 tsp. sesame oil

Gluten-free soy sauce (optional)

1 tbsp. toasted sesame seeds

1 Fill a medium saucepan halfway with water and bring water to a boil. Add beans to boiling water, reduce heat to simmer, and cook covered for 3 minutes.

2 While beans cook, heat canola oil over medium heat in a large skillet. Add garlic and sauté until fragrant and starting to brown. Reduce heat to low.

3 Drain water from beans. Add beans to skillet. Add a few dashes of sesame oil and gluten-free soy sauce. Stir until beans are coated with sauces and garlic. Stir in sesame seeds and serve.

SERVES 4

EFFORT Easy to make any day of the week

ACTIVE PREP 10 minutes

PAIRING Sauvignon Blanc or Omission Lager

TIP

Sauté 1 tbsp. of finely minced ginger with garlic to give this dish even more flavor.

Calories: 70; Total Fat (g): 3; Saturated Fat (g): 0; Cholesterol (mg): 0; Sodium (mg): 20; Potassium (mg): 180; Total Carbohydrate (g): 7; Fiber (g): 3; Sugar (g): 2; Protein (g): 2. Content per serving. Assumes 4 servings.

OVEN-ROASTED ASPARAGUS

Asparagus is a versatile veggie I try to prepare at least once a week. Even with as much as I use asparagus, and with as many preparation options as there are for it, I've found that nothing tops oven-roasting spears to crispy, succulent perfection. The roasting process confers a crunchy texture on the tips and keeps the stalks moist and tender. Simple and gourmet, this asparagus recipe can go with everything from steaks to salmon and Bordeaux to beer.

1 Preheat oven to 450 degrees and line baking sheet with foil.

2 Place asparagus in single layer on baking sheet.

3 Drizzle olive oil over spears and roll spears around to coat thoroughly. Sprinkle with salt and pepper. Bake for 15 minutes or until asparagus tips are slightly browned. Remove from oven and let rest for a minute before serving.

1 lb. asparagus spears, hard base snapped off

1 tbsp. extra virgin olive oil

¼ tsp. coarsely ground sea salt or kosher salt

¼ tsp. coarsely ground black pepper

SERVES 2 to 4
EFFORT Perfect for a work night
ACTIVE PREP 5 minutes
PAIRING Great as a side for my Spiced Salmon with Curry Dip recipe

TIP

To keep asparagus fresh, break off bases of spears immediately after purchase, then place spears in a tall, wide glass filled with about a half-inch of water (bottom end of spears placed in water) and store in the fridge.

Calories: 50; Total Fat (g): 4; Saturated Fat (g): 1; Cholesterol (mg): 0; Sodium (mg): 110; Potassium (mg): 230; Total Carbohydrate (g): 5; Fiber (g): 2; Sugar (g): 2; Protein (g): 2. Content per serving. Assumes 4 servings.

CRISPY STEAK FRIES

Has there ever been a more winning combination than steak and potatoes? Not to my way of thinking. It just works. For my take on this classic combo, I boil the potatoes first to get the insides soft and creamy and then bake them to get the outsides nice and crispy. This side is so superb that it can even be enjoyed in the absence of steak (though I can't conscionably recommend that!). I advise pairing it with Michelle's Carne Asada and a red wine for a win-win-win.

2 large baking potatoes, peeled and sliced into large fry-size pieces (about 4 to 5 inches long and 1 inch thick)
Sea salt
2 tbsp. extra virgin olive oil

1 Preheat oven to 400 degrees.

2 In a medium saucepan, combine potatoes and a dash of sea salt. Add water until potatoes are covered by about an inch of water. Bring to a boil. Reduce heat to simmer and cook uncovered for 10 to 15 minutes or until potatoes are soft when poked with a fork. Remove and dry potatoes.

3 Place dried potatoes on a foil-lined baking sheet. Drizzle with olive oil and gently rub with fingers to coat, trying not to break potatoes apart. Season with sea salt to liking and bake for 20 to 25 minutes, turning halfway through cooking time. Potatoes are ready when outsides are lightly browned and crispy.

SERVES 4
EFFORT Easy enough to make any day of the week
ACTIVE PREP 5 minutes
PAIRING Michelle's Carne Asada and Fess Parker Pinot Noir

TIP

Thinly sliced potatoes will break apart when boiled, so it's okay to have thick slices.

Calories 150; Total Fat (g): 5; Saturated Fat (g): 1; Cholesterol (mg): 0; Sodium (mg): 150; Potassium (mg): 620; Total Carbohydrate (g): 23; Fiber (g): 2; Sugar (g): 1; Protein (g): 2. Content per serving. Assumes 4 servings.

SALT AND VINEGAR KALE CHIPS

When I first tried kale chips sold at the supermarket, I was intrigued but skeptical. Yes, the chips are delicious, but I can't justify paying so much for those tiny bags. So I figured out how to make my own. The trick to getting them just right is to make sure the kale leaves crisp but don't burn, which requires attention while they bake. I remove them from the oven just as they're browning. This recipe is a great way to incorporate calcium, vitamins, and antioxidants into your diet. Go bag-less!

1 Place oven rack about 10 inches from top. Preheat oven to 400 degrees. Line 2 baking sheets with foil and set aside.

2 Place kale leaves in a large salad bowl. Set aside.

3 Whisk together vinegar, mustard, salt, and pepper in a mixing bowl. Pour in olive oil, whisking continuously while pouring. Once mixed, pour mixture over kale leaves. Toss to coat and place in a single layer on baking sheets.

4 Bake for 10 to 15 minutes or until leaves are crisp but not burned (it's okay if some are slightly browned). Turn leaves halfway through cooking time. If using Parmesan, sprinkle on leaves just after turning at the halfway point. When crisp, remove kale from oven and allow to cool for 5 to 10 minutes before serving.

10 oz. chopped kale, stems removed

3 tbsp. white balsamic vinegar

2 tsp. Dijon mustard

¼ tsp. sea salt

¼ tsp. ground black pepper

¼ cup olive oil

Aged Grated Parmesan cheese or lactose-free Parmesan

SERVES 2 to 4
EFFORT Easy
ACTIVE PREP 5 minutes
PAIRING Omission IPA

TIP

For Paleo prep, omit Parmesan. For vegan prep, use GO Veggie! Grated Parmesan.

Calories: 100; Total Fat (g): 8; Saturated Fat (g): 1; Cholesterol (mg): 0; Sodium (mg): 170; Potassium (mg): 310; Total Carbohydrate (g): 7; Fiber (g): 1; Sugar (g): 1; Protein (g): 3. Content per serving. Assumes 4 servings.

SPICY BROCCOLI

When preparing crucifers or other green vegetables, my go-to cooking technique is steaming because it's easy and quick. But when an entrée calls for a different texture, I'll swap out steaming for roasting. This recipe for roasted broccoli helps the veggie's flavors come alive and provides a slightly crunchy texture, while crushed red pepper flakes pack heat without fuss. Because of the strong flavors of this preparation, pair this side dish with a mildly flavored entrée, such as grilled chicken.

1 lb. broccoli, cut into florets
2 tbsp. extra virgin olive oil
Salt
Ground black pepper
Crushed red pepper flakes

SERVES 4
EFFORT Easy enough to make and spice up any meal any night
ACTIVE PREP 5 minutes
PAIRING Grilled chicken breasts, rice, and gluten-free beer

1 Preheat oven to 425 degrees.

2 Line baking sheet with foil and place broccoli on baking sheet. Drizzle with olive oil and toss to coat. Season with salt, black pepper, and crushed red pepper flakes to taste. (Note: A little crushed red pepper goes a long way!)

3 Bake for 15 minutes or until outsides of broccoli are starting to brown. Stir broccoli halfway through cooking time. Serve.

TIP

The flavonoids in broccoli and capsaicin in red pepper flakes are both noted anti-inflamatory agents. Turn the heat up on inflammation with this recipe!

Calories: 80; Total Fat (g): 7; Saturated Fat (g): 1; Cholesterol (mg): 0; Sodium (mg): 130; Potassium (mg): 230; Total Carbohydrate (g): 4; Fiber (g): 0; Sugar (g): 0; Protein (g): 2. Content per serving. Assumes 4 servings.

PIEROGI MASH

When I was growing up, my Polish grandparents used to make the best homemade pierogis. The potato and cheese-filled dumplings, served with sautéed onion, sour cream, and homemade sausage on the side, were incredibly savory and comforting. While making homemade pierogis can be a day-long event, this recipe can be whipped together in under 30 minutes. Despite its ease of preparation, this dish retains the wonderful flavors of my family's homemade pierogis.

3 to 4 medium baking potatoes, peeled and sliced crosswise into ¼-inch thick rounds

1 to 2 tbsp. lactose-free butter

Salt

Ground black pepper

1 small yellow onion, diced and sautéed in 1 tbsp. butter

3 to 4 tbsp. farmers cheese

1 Place potatoes in a medium-sized saucepan and add water until potatoes are just covered. Place on stovetop over high heat. Bring water to a boil. Reduce heat and simmer for 10 to 15 minutes, until potatoes are soft and ready to break apart when pierced with a fork.

2 Drain water, leaving potatoes in saucepan. Add butter and season with salt and pepper to taste. Mash.

3 Stir in sautéed onion and farmers cheese and mash until cheese and onions are evenly dispersed. Serve.

SERVES 6 to 8
EFFORT Easy enough to make on a weeknight
ACTIVE PREP 20 to 25 minutes
PAIRING Polish sausage and sauerkraut

TIP

Farmers cheese is a low-fat, low-lactose cheese and is typically well-tolerated even by those with digestive issues such as Crohn's disease or colitis (my husband tolerates it perfectly). Lactose-free cream cheese or lactose-free cottage cheese may be substituted in an equal quantity if desired.

Calories: 180; Total Fat (g): 3; Saturated Fat (g): 1; Cholesterol (mg): 4; Sodium (mg): 40; Potassium (mg): 830; Total Carbohydrate (g): 33; Fiber (g): 4; Sugar (g): 3; Protein (g): 5. Content per serving. Assumes 8 servings.

CAULIFLOWER PASTA

Roasted cauliflower is a fantastic gluten-free substitute for pasta, and it works particularly well as a side when paired with virtually any meat entree. Oven-roasted cauliflower seasoned with garlic and olive oil stands up to the flavors of beef and lamb, but also pairs well with baked fish. Either way, this recipe evokes the flavors of the Italian countryside and promises lightness where traditional noodles might be too filling. Enjoy whenever a meal could benefit from a few extra veggies. *Mangia!*

1 head of cauliflower, chopped into bite-size florets

3 tbsp. extra virgin olive oil

Salt

Ground black pepper

Red pepper flakes

6 cloves garlic, crushed

1 zucchini, thinly sliced into rounds

1 yellow onion, thinly sliced

4 oz. crimini mushrooms, thinly sliced

⅓ cup aged Parmesan or lac-tose-free Parmesan, grated

1 lemon, quartered

SERVES 4 to 6
EFFORT Requires some time
ACTIVE PREP 35 minutes
PAIRING Pinot Grigio

1 Preheat oven to 450 degrees. Place cauliflower in a glass baking dish, drizzle with 2 tbsp. olive oil and toss to coat. Sprinkle with salt, pepper, and red pepper flakes. Add garlic and toss again to coat. Bake for 25 minutes, stirring halfway through cooking time.

2 Heat a large, non-stick skillet over medium to medium-high heat. Add 1 tbsp. olive oil and swirl to coat. Once olive oil is warm, add zucchini, onion, and mushrooms. Sauté until vegetables have lost their firmness, about 5 to 7 minutes. Season with salt, pepper, and red pepper flakes to liking.

3 When cauliflower is ready, sprinkle with Parmesan. Set oven to broil and broil cauliflower until tops are starting to brown, about 2 to 3 minutes.

4 Remove cauliflower from oven, serve in small bowls, and top with sautéed vegetable mixture. Squeeze lemon juice on top. Add cheese, black pepper, and red pepper flakes to taste. Serve.

TIP

For a milder preparation, substitute ½ to 1 tbsp. chopped parsley for red pepper flakes. Add to cauliflower just before broiling. Omit cheese for Paleo prep.

Calories: 100; Total Fat (g): 8; Saturated Fat (g): 1; Cholesterol (mg): 2; Sodium (mg): 60; Potassium (mg): 270; Total Carbohydrate (g): 6; Fiber (g): 1; Sugar (g): 2; Protein (g): 2. Content per serving. Assumes 6 servings.

Butternut squash is one of those vegetables that tastes so good it's hard to believe it's healthy. In fact, when prepared using my recipe, squash could be dessert (if not for all the nutrition)! Serve this dish as a sweet side or mix it into salad or pasta. It's also great with bacon or sausage for a delight that covers both sweet and salty territory. Regardless, this side is monumentally easy to prepare and fills your kitchen with sweet cinnamon aromas that go hand in hand with autumn.

1 Preheat oven to 350 degrees and line a baking sheet with parchment paper.

2 In a small bowl, mix butter and olive oil. Place butternut squash cubes in a large, shallow dish. Pour butter and olive oil mixture over squash and toss to coat thoroughly.

3 Place butternut squash in a single layer on baking sheet. Sprinkle evenly with desired amounts of salt and pepper. Sprinkle brown sugar and cinnamon on top. Bake until squash is soft when poked with a fork and is beginning to caramelize, about 1 hour.

4 Sprinkle squash with pistachios and serve.

1 tbsp. lactose-free butter, melted
1 tbsp. extra virgin olive oil
1 lb. butternut squash, peeled and cut into 1-inch cubes
Salt
Ground black pepper
2 tbsp. brown sugar or palm sugar
½ tsp. cinnamon
¼ cup pistachios, finely chopped

TIP
For vegan prep, use Earth Balance Natural Buttery Spread.

SERVES 4 to 6
EFFORT Very easy
ACTIVE PREP 10 to 15 minutes
PAIRING Pork or sausage

Calories: 110; Total Fat (g): 7; Saturated Fat (g): 1; Cholesterol (mg): 0; Sodium (mg): 20; Potassium (mg): 320; Total Carbohydrate (g): 14; Fiber (g): 2; Sugar (g): 6; Protein (g): 2. Content per serving. Assumes 6 servings.

SUMMER VEGETABLE MEDLEY

In the summertime, I love pairing my summer vegetable medley with grilled salmon or steak. Light and fun to eat, this mélange makes a great side for a hearty filet of meat. And it's a breeze to make. Season the vegetables with garlic and herbs and roast them in the oven or grill them – wherever the filets are cooking. In addition to its painless preparation, the thing I love most about this recipe is that leftovers can be eaten chilled, which means zero prep later. Ease + Summertime = Bliss.

1 Move oven rack about 6 inches from the top and preheat oven to 400 degrees.

2 Bring a large pot of water to a boil. While water heats, fill a large bowl with cold water.

3 When water reaches boil, add carrots and cook until tender, about 10 minutes. Remove carrots from pot with tongs and place in cold water bath to prevent further cooking. Once carrots have cooled for about 1 minute, place them on a paper towel to dry.

4 Place zucchini and squash in boiling water and cook until tender, about 5 minutes. Remove from pot, place in cold water bath for about 1 minute, and dry on a paper towel.

5 Place carrots, squash, and zucchini on a baking sheet.

6 Whisk together remaining ingredients. Pour mixture over vegetables and toss to coat. Arrange vegetables in single layer.

7 Roast vegetables until they begin to brown slightly, about 10 to 15 minutes. Serve.

3 large carrots, peeled and chopped diagonally into 2-inch long rounds

3 medium zucchini, cut into ½-inch rounds

2 medium yellow squash, cut into ½-inch rounds

1 garlic clove, minced

1 to 2 tbsp. extra virgin olive oil

¼ tsp. smoked paprika

¼ tsp. dried rosemary

¼ tsp. ground black pepper

¼ tsp. or less salt

SERVES 4 to 6
EFFORT Easy to make but takes a while to cook
ACTIVE PREP 25 minutes
PAIRING Clean Slate Riesling

TIP
Serve leftovers atop cooked spaghetti noodles and toss with extra virgin olive oil and lemon juice. Season to taste with salt and ground black pepper.

Calories: 60; Total Fat (g): 2; Saturated Fat (g): 0; Cholesterol (mg): 0; Sodium (mg): 120; Potassium (mg): 530; Total Carbohydrate (g): 9; Fiber (g): 3; Sugar (g): 4; Protein (g): 2. Content per serving. Assumes 6 servings.

This recipe turns raw, bitter kale into a lightly-crisped, crave-worthy treat. Simple to prepare and easier on the palate than anything as healthy as kale ever should be, this recipe is a standby in my kitchen. No need to remove stems for this dish, it's ready in minutes. Which means it comes to the rescue on nights when you're pressed for time and running on empty.

1 Preheat oven to 400 degrees and line a baking sheet with foil.

2 In a large, deep skillet, bring about 1 inch of water to a boil. Add kale, reduce heat to low, cover, and cook for 3 minutes.

3 Drain kale in colander and run cold water over leaves. Dry with paper towels. It's okay if leaves remain slightly damp.

4 Place kale on baking sheet. Drizzle with olive oil, season with salt and pepper to taste, and toss to coat evenly. Arrange kale in a single layer.

5 Bake for 10 to 15 minutes, or until edges of leaves crisp, stirring occasionally. Serve.

10 oz. chopped kale
1 tbsp. extra virgin olive oil
Salt
Ground black pepper

SERVES 2 to 4
EFFORT Easy enough to whip together most any time
ACTIVE PREP 10 to 15 minutes
PAIRING Pairs well with almost any meat dish

TIP

Kale may also be baked in a glass dish. If prepared this way, baking may require 5 to 10 additional minutes.

Calories: 60; Total Fat (g): 4; Saturated Fat (g): 1; Cholesterol (mg): 0; Sodium (mg): 30; Potassium (mg): 310; Total Carbohydrate (g): 6; Fiber (g): 1; Sugar (g): 0; Protein (g): 3. Content per serving. Assumes 6 servings.

TERIYAKI BROCCOLI

If you're looking to jazz up dinner with a healthy crowd-pleaser, casting is closed. My teriyaki broccoli fills the bill and tastes great served warm or chilled. The flavors evoke favorite Asian dishes but without gluten, dairy, or MSG. Which means this dish is decidedly more in the tradition of Carnegie Hall than The Gong Show. For this side, I like to use Annie Chun's Gluten Free Teriyaki since it's relatively low in sodium. My teriyaki broccoli receives a standing ovation anytime it's called on stage.

1 lb. broccoli, chopped into bite-size florets
2 tbsp. gluten-free teriyaki sauce
1 tsp. lactose-free butter, melted
¼ cup cashews

1 Add water to a large skillet until water is about 1 inch deep. Bring water to a boil. Once boiling, add broccoli, cover, and cook until blanched, about 60 to 90 seconds.

2 Drain water from skillet, stir in teriyaki sauce, butter, and cashews. Heat skillet over medium heat and stir until broccoli is thoroughly coated with seasoning and heated through, about 2 minutes. Remove from heat and serve. May also be served at room temperature or chilled.

SERVES 4
EFFORT Easy to make any day of the week
ACTIVE PREP 10 minutes
PAIRING Sauvignon Blanc

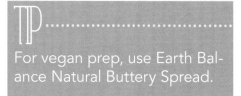

For vegan prep, use Earth Balance Natural Buttery Spread.

Calories: 100; Total Fat (g): 7; Saturated Fat (g): 1; Cholesterol (mg): 0; Sodium (mg): 200; Potassium (mg): 170; Total Carbohydrate (g): 7; Fiber (g): 0; Sugar (g): 3; Protein (g): 3. Content per serving. Assumes 4 servings.

SPICY CORN ON THE COB

Summer just isn't complete without corn on the cob. Sweet and fun to munch on, it's perfect on a warm evening spent outdoors. While traditional butter and salt toppings can be satisfying, they can also be heavy. This recipe adds spice and substitutes fresh-squeezed lime juice for butter, a secret my friend Lalit shared with me. Lime enhances the corn's flavor just as butter would, but it's also light and refreshing. I didn't believe it until I tried it for myself. So don't take my word for it – give lime a try!

1 Bring a large pot of water to a boil.

2 Insert corncobs and boil for 5 to 7 minutes or until the color of the corn darkens slightly.

3 Remove cobs from water and drizzle the juice of one quarter lime on each cob. Season with salt, pepper, and paprika to liking. Serve immediately.

4 ears fresh corncobs, shucked
1 lime, quartered
Salt
Ground black pepper
Smoked paprika

SERVES 4 to 8
EFFORT Easy
ACTIVE PREP 10 minutes
PAIRING My Cherry.Lemon.Martini

TIP

If you're feeling adventurous, try adding other herbs and spices such as chopped cilantro or chili powder.

Calories: 60; Total Fat (g): 1; Saturated Fat (g): 0; Cholesterol (mg): 0; Sodium (mg): 10; Potassium (mg): 60; Total Carbohydrate (g): 13; Fiber (g): 1; Sugar (g): 0; Protein (g): 2. Content per serving. Assumes 8 serving yield.

SOUTHERN HOSPITALITY SWEET POTATO FRIES

During a summer spent living in Atlanta, I loved going out to eat. I don't know if it was the Southern cooking or Southern hospitality that made eating out so great. But I do know that no meal was complete without sweet potato fries, which I'd snap up at every opportunity. Though the fries in this recipe aren't deep fried in true Southern style, they pack much of the same flavor and fun, and they're versatile enough to complement everything from burgers to blackened halibut.

2 to 3 medium to large sweet potatoes, sliced into fry-size pieces (about 3 to 4 inches long and ¼ inch thick), skin left on
2 tbsp. extra virgin olive oil
¼ tsp. sea salt
¼ tsp. ground black pepper
Smoked paprika

1 Move oven rack about 7 to 10 inches from top and preheat oven to 425 degrees.

2 Place potatoes in a glass baking dish or on a foil-lined baking sheet and drizzle with olive oil. Toss to coat. Add salt and pepper to potatoes and toss again. Sprinkle with paprika to taste before placing in oven.

3 Bake potatoes for 25 to 30 minutes, flipping and stirring halfway through cooking time. Fries are ready when centers are soft when poked with a fork and outsides are slightly crisped.

4 Allow fries to cool for a couple of minutes. Serve plain or with ketchup, mustard, or mayo.

SERVES 4 to 6
EFFORT Easy enough to make on a weeknight
ACTIVE PREP 5 minutes
PAIRING Serve with burgers or any grilled, baked, or skillet-cooked meat

TIP For added flavor, sprinkle fries with lactose-free Parmesan or aged, grated Parmesan for low-lactose prep.

Calories: 100; Total Fat (g): 5; Saturated Fat (g): 1; Cholesterol (mg): 0; Sodium (mg): 110; Potassium (mg): 220; Total Carbohydrate (g): 13; Fiber (g): 2; Sugar (g): 3; Protein (g): 1. Content per serving. Assumes 6 servings.

GARLIC BROCCOLINI

When I'm looking for an easy way to prepare a leafy green side, I go to my garlic broccolini recipe. Like a faithful sidekick who's ready for action anytime the going gets tough, this side can be whipped together in a matter of minutes, even under the most trying of circumstances. And like any good sidekick, there's much more than meets the eye. This broccolini packs a punch of flavor and heroic healthiness to boot. If you like your sidekicks hot, replace paprika with a dash of red pepper flakes.

8 oz. broccolini, trimmed and leaves removed
1 tbsp. extra virgin olive oil
1 tbsp. lactose-free butter
6 garlic cloves, thinly sliced
Salt
Smoked paprika or red pepper flakes

1 In a large, shallow skillet, bring ¼ cup water to a boil. When water reaches boil, reduce heat to low or medium-low, add broccolini, cover, and cook for 2 minutes. Drain water, remove broccolini, and set aside on a plate.

2 Heat olive oil and butter in skillet over medium heat. Add garlic and sauté until fragrant and starting to brown. Return broccolini to skillet and sauté until warm and coated with garlic mixture, about 1 to 2 minutes.

3 Sprinkle with salt and smoked paprika or red pepper flakes (if using) and serve.

SERVES 2 to 4
EFFORT Easy to make any day of the week
ACTIVE PREP 10 minutes
PAIRING Marques de Riscal Reserva

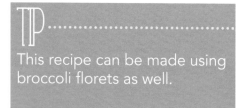

This recipe can be made using broccoli florets as well.

Calories: 80; Total Fat (g): 6; Saturated Fat (g): 1; Cholesterol (mg): 0; Sodium (mg): 70; Potassium (mg): 40; Total Carbohydrate (g): 3; Fiber (g): 0; Sugar (g): 1; Protein (g): 1. Content per serving. Assumes 4 servings.

BREAKFAST

It's said that breakfast is the most important meal of the day, and that's not something I doubt. The trouble is that, as important as breakfast may be, it can also be awfully boring!

If there's one meal each day where I tend to fall into tedium and redundancy, it's the meal that gets squeezed in between sleep and everything else. Those wee hours are rushed, regardless of whether it's the morning of a weekday chock full of meetings and deadlines or a weekend packed with errands and outings. These recipes are my favorite breakfast standbys, many of which easily fit just about any schedule and pack enough nutritional goodies that, no matter what your schedule holds, you're up to the challenge.

For days when you crave treats that are hard to find prepared without gluten and lactose, I've included a couple of fun recipes, such as Maple Bacon Doughnuts and Orange Pistachio Muffins. Now breakfast doesn't have to just be important – it can be easy, fun, and tasty, too!

COCONUT DATE OATMEAL

In recognition of the health benefits of coconut, chia seeds, and dates, I put these inflammation and oxidation ninjas together in a powerhouse breakfast that ensures I'm ready to square off against the day. My coconut date oatmeal is fast and easy to make, delicious and invigorating, and ruthless against unwanted free radicals – the perfect way to jump-start a morning. Give this coconut date oatmeal a try anytime you need a bit more kick or an extra punch of flavor to begin your day.

½ cup gluten-free rolled oats

1 cup water or soy milk (I recommend using half of each)

¼ crisp, sweet apple, finely chopped (Opal apple, if in season)

1 date, pit removed and chopped

1 tsp. honey

1 tsp. orange juice

2 to 3 walnuts, finely chopped

1 tbsp. sweetened, shaved coconut flakes

¼ tsp. chia seeds

1 Prepare oats according to package instructions, using water and/or soy milk as desired.

2 When oatmeal is cooked, add apple, date, honey, and orange juice. Stir.

3 Sprinkle chopped walnuts, coconut flakes, and chia seeds on top of oatmeal. Serve immediately.

TIP

This recipe tastes great cold too. Omit orange juice, stir in remaining ingredients, and serve with cold, lactose-free milk.

SERVES 1

EFFORT Easy enough to make, eat, and clean up before the morning commute

ACTIVE PREP 5 minutes

PAIRING Fresh-squeezed orange juice and coffee

Calories: 390; Total Fat (g): 11; Saturated Fat (g): 3; Cholesterol (mg): 0; Sodium (mg): 80; Potassium (mg): 400; Total Carbohydrate (g): 69; Fiber (g): 9; Sugar (g): 35; Protein (g): 11. Content per serving. Assumes 1 serving.

THE PENELOPE SANDWICH

To help avoid a weekend morning that feels like it belongs to a weekday, I look for a breakfast that promises lazy hours with the newspaper. The Penelope signals weekend relaxation like nothing else. Simple enough to make that it won't preclude the Sunday crossword, but unique and delectable enough to be a treat, the Penelope is at its best when paired with Saturday and Sunday R & R. What's an eight-letter synonym for delicious that starts with "P"?

1 Heat a non-stick skillet over medium heat. Add olive oil and swirl to coat. Once oil is warm, pour beaten eggs into skillet. Do not scramble eggs. Shake pan to help eggs settle into a single layer and use spatula to lift edges to avoid sticking. Cook for about 1 to 2 minutes. When bottom side of eggs is cooked, flip over and continue cooking for another 1 to 2 minutes.

2 With eggs still in skillet, sprinkle cheddar in a single layer atop one half of egg area. Top cheddar with bacon slices. Fold other half of the eggs over bacon and cheddar, turn heat to medium-low, and continue cooking until cheddar has melted.

3 Spread butter on bagels.

4 Divide egg mixture in half with spatula and place on bagels, forming sandwiches. Serve.

1 to 2 tsp. extra virgin olive oil

4 eggs, beaten

¼ cup lactose-free shredded cheddar

2 slices bacon, prepared according to package instructions

1 tbsp. lactose-free butter

2 gluten-free bagels, toasted

TIP ·······················
For low-lactose preparation, I recommend using Trader Joe's X-tra X-tra Sharp New York Cheddar Cheese.

Calories: 280; Total Fat (g): 16; Saturated Fat (g): 3; Cholesterol (mg): 220; Sodium (mg): 500; Potassium (mg): 80; Total Carbohydrate (g): 24; Fiber (g): 1; Sugar (g): 3; Protein (g): 12. Content per serving. Assumes 4 servings.

SERVES 2 to 4
EFFORT The Penelope's natural habitat is the weekend - straightforward to make but takes some time
ACTIVE PREP 15 to 20 minutes
PAIRING Fresh-squeezed orange juice and coffee

ORGANIC BERRY CHERRY SMOOTHIE

Getting enough fruit into your diet can feel like a full-time job. I often reach the end of the day and realize I've had only a fraction of the fruit I should have eaten. Then, when I check the fridge, I find the fruit I bought for the week has gone bad! Now I stock frozen berries for blending smoothies. Cool, sweet, and refreshing, this smart smoothie is an easy way to help get in your day's worth of fruit. Chia adds omega-3s, protein, and thickness to this "berry" delicious beverage – all without any lactose.

1 Blend ingredients together until smooth, about 1 minute.

2 Pour into glass and serve immediately.

1 heaping cup frozen organic mixed berries, thawed at room temperature for 5 to 10 minutes

2 oz. fresh-squeezed orange juice

2 oz. cherry juice

½ tbsp. chia seeds

½ tsp. vanilla extract (optional)

1 ripe banana (optional)

SERVES 1 to 2

EFFORT Easy enough to make before you head out for work. Pour in a to-go cup to enjoy during your morning commute.

ACTIVE PREP 5 minutes

PAIRING My Granola-To-Goji

TIP

Try adding a little coconut yogurt to give this blend a creamy, tropical taste! After a workout, I like to add a scoop of vanilla protein powder to my smoothie.

Calories: 140; Total Fat (g): 3; Saturated Fat (g): 0; Cholesterol (mg): 0; Sodium (mg): 30; Potassium (mg): 230; Total Carbohydrate (g): 16; Fiber (g): 6; Sugar (g): 18; Protein (g): 3. Content per serving. Assumes 2 servings.

HUEVOS ROTOS

Huevos rotos or "broken eggs" is the Spanish term for fried eggs set atop potato fries. While huevos rotos can be enjoyed any time of day, they make an especially satisfying breakfast. My take on this dish calls for potatoes to be oven-baked rather than fried and for modest use of salt. This recipe also provides a good "base" that can be easily modified. For example, huevos rotos can be transformed into a sophisticated delight by serving quail eggs atop truffle fries.

6 to 8 new potatoes, sliced into wedges or "fry-shaped" pieces

1 to 2 tbsp. extra virgin olive oil

Salt

Ground black pepper

2 oz. Spanish ham or chorizo, chopped

1 tbsp. canola oil

4 eggs

1 Preheat oven to 425 degrees. Place potatoes in a glass baking dish. Drizzle with olive oil and toss to coat, then season with salt and pepper to taste. Bake for 30 minutes, stirring potatoes halfway through cooking time. Centers of potatoes should be soft and edges slightly crispy and browned when ready.

2 When potatoes have about 5 minutes of cooking time left, top with ham or chorizo and continue cooking. Remove potatoes and meat from oven when cooked and divide among serving plates.

3 Heat canola oil in a non-stick skillet over medium to medium-high heat and fry eggs (either sunny-side up or over easy). Serve eggs atop potatoes and meat. Enjoy.

SERVES 2 to 4
EFFORT Better to make on a weekend
ACTIVE PREP 10 to 15 minutes
PAIRING Fresh-squeezed orange juice and café

TIP

Just before eating this dish, break the egg yolks open and toss with potatoes and meat using a fork and knife for the complete "broken eggs" experience.

Calories: 370; Total Fat (g): 17; Saturated Fat (g): 3; Cholesterol (mg): 223; Sodium (mg): 360; Potassium (mg): 1150; Total Carbohydrate (g): 41; Fiber (g): 4; Sugar (g): 2; Protein (g): 15. Content per serving. Assumes 4 servings.

FRENCH TOAST CASSEROLE

When hosting an extended-family overnight gathering, ensuring that everyone receives an adequate breakfast can be a challenge. Add time zone differences, kids, pets, etc. and that challenge quickly morphs into catastrophe. This dish is great for family breakfasts and entertaining. That's because this casserole is prepared the night before serving, so day-of prep simply entails popping it in the oven. And the scent of sweet cinnamon gets heavy sleepers out of bed before noon!

1 Lightly butter one side of each slice of bread and set aside.

2 In a large bowl, whisk together eggs, milk, vanilla extract, and powdered sugar. Set aside.

3 In a separate bowl, combine brown/palm sugar, granulated sugar, cinnamon, and nutmeg. Set aside.

4 Place a layer of bread, butter side down, in a 9-by-13-inch baking dish. Spoon ½ of egg mixture over top of bread slices, then sprinkle with ½ of spice mix and add a dusting of powdered sugar. Add a second layer of bread slices with butter side up this time. Spoon remaining egg mixture on top and sprinkle with remaining spices and powdered sugar. Cover with foil and refrigerate overnight.

5 In the morning, preheat oven to 350 degrees, remove cover from casserole, and bake until bread is golden, about 35 to 40 minutes. Serve immediately. Drizzle with maple syrup as desired.

Lactose-free butter

1 loaf gluten-free bread

6 large eggs

1½ cups lactose-free milk

1 tsp. vanilla extract

1 tbsp. powdered sugar + extra for dusting layers of casserole

1 tbsp. brown sugar or palm sugar

1 tbsp. granulated sugar

½ tsp. cinnamon

½ tsp. nutmeg

Maple syrup

SERVES 6 to 8
EFFORT Easy enough to prepare any night and bake the next morning
ACTIVE PREP 15 minutes
PAIRING Fresh-squeezed juice and coffee

TIP

Place a slice of bacon on each serving dish and place casserole on top. The sweet and salty combination of French toast and bacon gives this dish extra "wow" factor.

Calories: 250; Total Fat (g): 7; Saturated Fat (g): 2; Cholesterol (mg): 161; Sodium (mg): 200; Potassium (mg): 100; Total Carbohydrate (g): 36; Fiber (g): 2; Sugar (g): 9; Protein (g): 9. Content per serving. Assumes 8 servings.

PEANUT BUTTER OATMEAL

I love peanut butter. I talk about it more than I ought to. I eat it every chance I get. And I cook with it whenever I can. Afterall, it's high in protein, fiber, vitamins, minerals, and monounsaturated fat. It's even been linked to decreased risk of diabetes. It also adds a lot of oomph to your morning meal. I've combined peanut butter and oatmeal here for a healthy and filling breakfast that gives you the fuel you'll need for a great day.

½ cup gluten-free rolled oats, prepared according to package instructions

1 cup water

1 to 2 tbsp. creamy peanut butter

1 tsp. honey

Salt

1 After heating oats, add peanut butter, honey, and a dash of sea salt. Stir vigorously.

2 Let rest for 1 to 2 minutes before eating to allow oatmeal to cool and soak up flavors.

SERVES 1
EFFORT This is a great meal before work or school
ACTIVE PREP 5 minutes
PAIRING Grape or cherry juice

TIP

Sprinkle chia seeds or flax meal in oatmeal to add omega-3s. Other toppings, like jam, can be fun as well.

Calories: 310; Total Fat (g): 15; Saturated Fat (g): 3; Cholesterol (mg): 0; Sodium (mg): 60; Potassium (mg): 150; Total Carbohydrate (g): 39; Fiber (g): 6; Sugar (g): 9; Protein (g): 11. Content per serving. Assumes 1 serving.

There's often a tradeoff when it comes to breakfast: either the meal provides enough energy to get you through the day (but leaves you feeling stuffed), or it's light enough that you're not too full (but leaves you hungry and depleted long before lunchtime). This egg and veggie quinoa recipe eliminates the tradeoff, providing instant energy and long-lasting reserves without the weight. This meal is easy to enjoy, and it packs flavor, omega-3s, and plenty of veggies.

1 Place lettuce leaves in bottom of a bowl. Top with avocado and then with warm quinoa, asparagus, tomato, and walnuts.

2 Place fried egg on top and season to taste with salt, pepper, and a drizzle of olive oil. Serve immediately. Break egg yolk over top before eating.

Handful of baby romaine lettuce leaves

½ avocado, diced

½ cup dry red quinoa, prepared according to package instructions

3 to 4 asparagus spears, steamed and chopped into 2-inch long pieces

3 to 4 mini heirloom tomatoes, halved

1 to 2 tbsp. chopped walnuts

2 eggs, cooked sunny side up

Salt

Ground black pepper

Extra virgin olive oil

TIP

Cucumber-lime infused water goes great with this dish. To make, place several slices of cucumber and 1 lime sliced into rounds in a Mason jar. Fill with water, seal, and refrigerate overnight. Serve over ice.

Calories: 300; Total Fat (g): 20; Saturated Fat (g): 3; Cholesterol (mg): 215; Sodium (mg): 80; Potassium (mg): 590; Total Carbohydrate (g): 22; Fiber (g): 7; Sugar (g): 5; Protein (g): 11. Content per serving. Assumes 2 servings.

SERVES 2
EFFORT Too involved for a weekday unless the quinoa and asparagus are prepared ahead of time
ACTIVE PREP 25 to 30 minutes
PAIRING Cucumber-lime infused water

FRUIT TEA CUP

When I stayed at a bed and breakfast in California wine country, the breakfast starter was a fruit salad in tea. I'll admit skepticism at first, but that doubt was quickly erased by the sweet and subtle flavors of the dish. It was such a refreshing treat that I decided to create my own version. This fruit concoction is great any time of day and a wonderful way to spice up typical fruit salad. Though nice at breakfast, it's also great after a meal, cleansing the palate and aiding in digestion.

¼ to ½ apple, diced

10 to 12 grapes, halved

2 servings mint tea or ginger pear tea, brewed and chilled for at least 4 hours

2 to 3 mint leaves, finely chopped

1 Place fruit in a glass serving dish or cup. Pour tea over fruit until just covered.

2 Sprinkle mint leaves on top and serve immediately. Use a spoon to scoop out fruit and tea.

SERVES 2

EFFORT Easy enough to make any time

ACTIVE PREP 5 to 10 minutes

PAIRING Serve as a breakfast starter or enjoy as a light dessert

TIP

Try different combinations, like cucumbers and lime juice with mint tea or apples and oranges with apple cinnamon herbal tea.

Calories: 40; Total Fat (g): 0; Saturated Fat (g): 0; Cholesterol (mg): 0; Sodium (mg): 0; Potassium (mg): 80; Total Carbohydrate (g): 9; Fiber (g): 1; Sugar (g): 7; Protein (g): 0. Content per serving. Assumes 2 servings.

CHOCOLATE CHIP OATMEAL BARS

Since I work out first thing in the morning, I like to have a snack bar before heading out for a run or to the gym. While store-bought snack bars are a good option, they can be expensive and high in processed sugars and sodium. These oatmeal bars are a healthy alternative to store-bought energy bars. Great as pre-workout fuel or grab-n-go breakfast, they're the perfect way to roll some cholesterol-lowering oats into your diet and kick your calorie-busting workouts into high gear.

1 tbsp. lactose-free butter, softened

2 tbsp. brown sugar or palm sugar

1 egg, lightly beaten

½ tsp. vanilla extract

¼ tsp. salt

1 cup gluten-free rolled oats

¼ cup semi-sweet chocolate chips

8 Medjool dates, pits removed and finely chopped

1 scoop gluten-free, lactose-free vanilla protein mix (optional)

SERVES 4
EFFORT Easy to make even if you're in a hurry to hit the treadmill
ACTIVE PREP 10 to 15 minutes
PAIRING Juice, lactose-free milk, and/or coffee

1 Preheat oven to 350 degrees. Line a baking sheet with foil and set aside.

2 Mix butter and sugar together in a large bowl. Stir in egg, vanilla extract, and salt. Slowly stir in oats, chocolate chips, dates, and protein mix (if using).

3 Lightly grease foil with a touch of butter. Spread oat mixture evenly on foil, creating a ½-inch deep rectangle measuring about 4-by-8-inches. Bake until edges are browned, about 10 minutes.

4 Remove from oven and allow mixture to cool for 5 to 10 minutes. Slice into four snack bars, each measuring about 4-by-2-inches. Serve immediately or store in a sealed container in a cool, dry place.

TIP

For vegan preparation, use vegan chocolate chips and vegan butter. Replace egg with 1 tbsp. flax meal soaked in 3 tbsp. water for 5 minutes.

Calories: 350; Total Fat (g): 9; Saturated Fat (g): 4; Cholesterol (mg): 54; Sodium (mg): 150; Potassium (mg): 350; Total Carbohydrate (g): 66; Fiber (g): 7; Sugar (g): 47; Protein (g): 6. Content per serving. Assumes 4 servings.

BREAKFAST BURRITO

When I have a long day ahead of me and I'm uncertain about the timing and contents of my next meal, I like to hit as many food groups at breakfast as I can. This breakfast burrito packs a healthy combination of protein, vegetables, fiber, and calcium, all rolled neatly together in a gluten-free tortilla. Add a glass of juice on the side, and you'll know you're starting your day off right...even if you're unsure where it'll go from there!

1 Heat a large non-stick skillet over medium-high to high heat and add 3 tbsp. water. When water begins to sizzle, add broccoli and cover for 2 minutes.

2 Drain water and return skillet with broccoli to burner and set to medium heat. Add olive oil, onions, mushrooms, and jalapeño. Sauté until onions begin to soften and mushrooms lose their firmness, about 3 to 5 minutes. Add tomatoes, spinach, and beans. Continue sautéing for about 1 minute. Season with pepper, paprika, chili powder, and salt.

3 Stir beaten eggs into mixture and continue cooking until eggs are cooked through. Turn off heat and let rest.

4 Place each tortilla on a microwave-safe plate, sprinkle with cheese, and heat one at a time in the microwave on high heat for 15 to 25 seconds, or until cheese has melted.

5 Scoop egg mixture into tortillas, wrap, and serve.

½ cup broccoli florets

2 tsp. extra virgin olive oil

½ cup yellow onion, diced

½ cup mushrooms, sliced

1 tbsp. jalapeño pepper, minced

½ cup tomatoes, diced

2 cups spinach leaves, stems removed

½ cup canned pinto beans, drained, rinsed, and dried

½ tsp. ground black pepper

½ tsp. smoked paprika

½ tsp. chili powder

¼ tsp. or less salt

8 eggs, 4 yolks discarded, beaten

2 to 4 rice flour tortillas

4 oz. lactose-free cheddar or aged, grated cheddar for low-lactose prep

Calories: 370; Total Fat (g): 17; Saturated Fat (g): 4; Cholesterol (mg): 430; Sodium (mg): 860; Potassium (mg): 1100; Total Carbohydrate (g): 34; Fiber (g): 8; Sugar (g): 2; Protein (g): 22. Content per serving. Assumes 4 servings.

SERVES 4

EFFORT Save this for mornings when you're not rushed

ACTIVE PREP 25 to 35 minutes

PAIRING Coffee and fruit juice

MAPLE BACON DOUGHNUTS

My husband and I are not big doughnut eaters, but when cravings have struck, we've been left floating without a go-to option. I created this recipe to come to the rescue. A true morning-time life preserver, these doughnuts breathe vigor into breakfast, with crispy, salty bacon, sweet maple, and soft, moist dough. While not a health food, it's hard to argue that these doughnuts don't make you feel more lively in the wee hours. Plus, aromas of maple fill the kitchen as they bake – perfect for fall!

DOUGHNUTS

Canola oil spray

1¼ cups cashew meal

1 tsp. cinnamon

½ tsp. nutmeg

¼ tsp. all spice

¼ tsp. gluten-free baking soda

¼ cup lactose-free butter, melted

2 large eggs

3 tbsp. maple syrup

2 tbsp. unsweetened applesauce

½ tsp. vanilla extract

MAPLE GLAZE

3 tbsp. confectioners sugar

1 tbsp. maple syrup

¼ tsp. vanilla extract

2 slices bacon, cooked and crumbled

1 Preheat oven to 350 degrees and spray a doughnut tray with canola oil.

2 In a large bowl, combine cashew meal, cinnamon, nutmeg, all spice, and baking soda into a dry mixture.

3 In a medium bowl, mix together butter, eggs, maple syrup, applesauce, and vanilla. Gradually stir wet mixture into dry mixture to create batter.

4 Spoon doughnut batter into tray, being careful not to fill doughnut cups more than ¾ full. Bake for 7 to 10 minutes or until cooked through. Let doughnuts cool.

5 Mix together glaze ingredients. Drizzle glaze over cooled doughnuts and sprinkle with bacon bits. Serve.

....

SERVES 6 to 9
EFFORT Surprisingly easy
ACTIVE PREP 10 to 15 minutes
PAIRING Coffee and lactose-free milk

TIP

For Paleo prep, substitute coconut oil for butter and use pure maple syrup and pure, unsweetened applesauce. Omit confectioners sugar.

Calories: 200; Total Fat (g): 13; Saturated Fat (g): 3; Cholesterol (mg): 50; Sodium (mg): 100; Potassium (mg): 130; Total Carbohydrate (g): 15; Fiber (g): 1; Sugar (g): 11; Protein (g): 5. Content per serving. Assumes 9 servings.

CHOCOLATE CASHEW OATMEAL BARS

Great as breakfast or as fuel before exercising, these bars incorporate oats, cashew butter, and honey. They're a yummy alternative to my Chocolate Chip Oatmeal Bars when the additional creaminess imparted by cashew butter is desired. These also satisfy a sweet tooth, which makes them great as a nighttime snack used to fend off less healthy desserts. Whenever they're enjoyed, this recipe's fiber, protein, and healthy fats will keep you feeling and looking as good as these bars taste.

1 egg, beaten

3 tbsp. lactose-free butter, softened

2 tbsp. brown sugar or palm sugar

1 tsp. honey

¼ cup semi-sweet chocolate chips

¼ cup chopped walnuts

¼ cup cashew butter (peanut butter may be substituted if desired)

¾ cup gluten-free rolled oats

SERVES 8

EFFORT Easy enough to make on a weekday

ACTIVE PREP 10 to 15 minutes

PAIRING Coffee, fruit juice, or coconut milk

1 Preheat oven to 350 degrees. Line baking sheet with foil and set aside.

2 Mix egg, butter, sugar, and honey in a large bowl. Stir in chocolate chips and walnuts. Stir in cashew butter until ingredients are combined. Gradually stir in oats.

3 Lightly grease foil with touch of butter. Spread oat mixture evenly on foil, creating a ½-inch deep rectangle measuring about 4-by-8-inches. Bake until edges are browned, about 10 minutes.

4 Remove from oven and allow mixture to cool for 5 to 10 minutes. Slice into eight squares, each measuring about 2-by-2-inches. Serve immediately or store in a sealed container in a cool, dry place.

TIP

For vegan preparation, use vegan chocolate chips and butter. Omit egg and replace with 1 tbsp. flax meal soaked in 3 tbsp. water for 5 minutes.

Calories: 220; Total Fat (g): 16; Saturated Fat (g): 4; Cholesterol (mg): 27; Sodium (mg): 50; Potassium (mg): 80; Total Carbohydrate (g): 17; Fiber (g): 2; Sugar (g): 8; Protein (g): 4. Content per serving. Assumes 8 servings.

ORANGE PISTACHIO MUFFINS

Pistachio gelato inspired this recipe. And every bit as much as the Italian *delizia* after which it's modeled, my orange pistachio muffin recipe enchants the taste buds. Orange zest and sugary crumbles add a sweet touch to these nutty, buttery muffins, which go perfectly alongside morning espresso. Like anything inspired by the Italians should be, my orange pistachio muffins are easy on the eyes, and their gluten-free, lactose-free texture and taste are pleasing on the palate.

MUFFINS

2 cups gluten-free all-purpose flour

¾ cup granulated sugar

½ cup pistachio pieces, finely chopped

2 tsp. gluten-free baking powder

1 tsp. xanthan gum

½ tsp. salt

¼ tsp. nutmeg

½ cup lactose-free butter, softened

½ cup lactose-free milk

2 eggs

½ cup fresh-squeezed orange juice

2 tsp. orange zest

1 tsp. vanilla extract

CRUMBLED SUGAR TOPPING

¼ cup gluten-free all-purpose flour

2 tbsp. lactose-free butter, softened

2 tbsp. granulated sugar

1 tsp. orange zest

¼ cup pistachio pieces, coarsely chopped

1 Preheat oven to 375 degrees and line a muffin pan with paper liners.

2 To make crumbled sugar topping, stir together flour, butter, sugar, and orange zest. Stir in pistachio pieces and set aside.

3 To make muffins, combine flour, sugar, pistachio pieces, baking powder, xanthan gum, salt, and nutmeg in a medium bowl.

4 In a large bowl, whisk together butter, milk, eggs, orange juice, orange zest, and vanilla extract. Stir flour mixture into liquid mixture until flour is just moistened, being careful not to over stir.

5 Pour muffin mixture into pan, filling cups about ¾ full. Top each muffin with a small amount of sugar topping. Bake for 10 minutes, then rotate tray. Continue baking until muffins are golden brown around the edges and a toothpick comes out clean when inserted in the center of a muffin, about 8 to 10 minutes. Cool in pan for 2 to 3 minutes. Serve or transfer to a wire cooling rack.

••••••••••••••••••••••••••••••••••••

SERVES 12 to 15
EFFORT Save for a weekend
ACTIVE PREP 30 to 35 minutes
PAIRING Coffee and lactose-free milk

Calories: 190; Total Fat (g): 11; Saturated Fat (g): 3; Cholesterol (mg): 29; Sodium (mg): 100; Potassium (mg): 100; Total Carbohydrate (g): 21; Fiber (g): 1; Sugar (g): 5; Protein (g): 3. Content per serving. Assumes 15 servings.

TIP

These muffins taste best if prepared when oranges are fresh and in season. For sweeter muffins, use an all-purpose flour with rice flour. For preparation without rice flour, Bob's Red Mill All-Purpose Flour works perfectly.

GRANOLA-TO-GOJI

Even on hectic days, I still try to eat right. It's on those crazy days when I couldn't survive without my granola recipe. Featuring rolled oats, coconut oil, chia seeds, and Himalayan superfruit goji berries, it's great for making during the weekend to be used as a weekday breakfast or a snack on the go. Because of its wholesome ingredients, my recipe packs long-lasting energy in low-glycemic style. Plus, it's more bang for the buck than store-bought granola. Get on the go with this granola!

3 cups gluten-free rolled oats
½ cup cashew meal
¼ cashew pieces
⅓ cup palm sugar
1 tbsp. chia seeds
1½ tsp. cinnamon
½ tsp. salt
¼ cup coconut oil
¾ cup goji berries

1 Preheat oven to 250 degrees and line 2 baking sheets with foil.

2 In a large bowl, combine oats, cashew meal, cashews, palm sugar, chia seeds, cinnamon, and salt. Stir.

3 Stir coconut oil into bowl. Pour mixture onto baking sheets.

4 Bake for 1 hour and 15 minutes, stirring every 15 minutes.

5 Remove granola from oven and allow to cool completely before pouring into a large bowl and stirring in goji berries. Serve or store covered in a cool, dry place.

SERVES 6
EFFORT Easy but requires over an hour for baking
ACTIVE PREP 10 minutes
PAIRING Lactose-free milk

TIP

For different flavor, try adding dried blueberries instead of goji berries or hemp seeds instead of chia seeds.

Calories: 430; Total Fat (g): 19; Saturated Fat (g): 10; Cholesterol (mg): 0; Sodium (mg): 200; Potassium (mg): 300; Total Carbohydrate (g): 56; Fiber (g): 8; Sugar (g): 21; Protein (g): 12. Content per serving. Assumes 6 servings.

I love dessert. My guilty pleasures include peanut butter, almond paste, ice cream, gelato (yes, I consider ice cream and gelato separate categories!), cupcakes, my friend Anne's pumpkin "whoopie" pies...the list goes on.

My husband, on the other hand, loves salty foods like tortilla chips and salsa, hot wings, barbecue...but can easily pass on sweets, which he argues are usually too sugary.

All of which would be fine except for the fact that, as much as I may love desserts, I just can't eat them alone. It seems irresponsible to do it by myself; I need a partner in crime.

With that in mind, I've developed some dessert recipes that satisfy my sweet tooth without being "too sweet" for my husband. While I wouldn't classify all these desserts as health foods, they aren't so packed with sugar or processed ingredients that you crash and burn after eating them or wake up the next day feeling (or looking) like a marshmallow.

ROASTED FIGS WITH WALNUTS AND HONEY

Greek mythology links figs with hospitality, and the connection makes sense: The sweet satisfaction of a fig makes anywhere feel welcoming. To accentuate figs' flavor, this recipe calls for oven-roasting them and adding toasted walnuts, honey, and crumbled bacon. The combination results in "fig-liciousness" of Herculean proportions. It's a dessert fit for the gods, with vitamins, amino acids, antioxidants, and flavor of an epic scale. Skip the ambrosia; stick with figs!

Lactose-free butter

8 to 10 fresh figs, halved length-wise

1 to 2 tbsp. brown sugar

¼ cup walnut pieces

1 slice bacon, cooked crispy and crumbled (optional)

Honey

1 Preheat oven to 400 degrees. Line baking sheet with foil.

2 Butter sliced side of figs and sprinkle with brown sugar.

3 Place figs buttered/sugared-side down on baking sheet and bake until figs are soft and browned on the bottom, about 10 to 15 minutes. When figs have about 3 to 5 minutes left to bake, place walnuts on baking sheet and continue baking. Walnuts should bake until they start to turn slightly golden brown on the outside.

4 Place figs in serving bowls with cut side facing up. Top with toasted walnuts and bacon (if using). Drizzle with honey. To really make the flavors pop, scrape the burnt sugar from the baking sheet and sprinkle atop figs.

SERVES 4

EFFORT Easy enough to make any time

ACTIVE PREP 10 to 15 minutes

PAIRING Serve on top of lactose-free vanilla ice cream

Calories: 230; Total Fat (g): 13; Saturated Fat (g): 2; Cholesterol (mg): 2; Sodium (mg): 70; Potassium (mg): 360; Total Carbohydrate (g): 31; Fiber (g): 4; Sugar (g): 25; Protein (g): 3. Content per serving. Assumes 4 servings.

CINNAMON RAISIN OATMEAL COOKIES

I'm a sucker for anything with cinnamon and sugar. Even something as simple as buttered toast with cinnamon and sugar I can't resist. But when gluten and lactose got eliminated from our diets, so did many cinnamon-sweet favorites. So I came up with this recipe to get the same great cinnamon and sugar taste without forbidden contents. Get ready for "cinn-fully" delicious flavor. And breathe deeply - your kitchen will smell great!

1 tbsp. flax meal

3 tbsp. water

3 tbsp. lactose-free butter, room temperature

4 tbsp. brown sugar or palm sugar

1 tbsp. granulated sugar

½ tsp. vanilla extract

¼ cup gluten-free all-purpose flour

½ tsp. ground cinnamon

¼ tsp. gluten-free baking soda

⅛ tsp. salt

1 heaping cup gluten-free rolled oats

¼ cup raisins

SERVES 12
EFFORT Easy enough to make any time
ACTIVE PREP 15 to 20 minutes
PAIRING Lactose-free milk

1 Preheat oven to 375 degrees. Combine flax meal and water in a small bowl and let stand for 5 minutes.

2 Combine butter with brown/palm sugar and granulated sugar in a large bowl. Stir in flax meal mixture and vanilla. Add flour, cinnamon, baking soda, and salt. Gradually stir in oats and raisins.

3 Drop rounded tablespoons of cookie mixture onto an ungreased cookie sheet. Mixture should yield about 12 cookies.

4 Bake for 8 to 10 minutes or until edges of cookies are slightly browned. Allow cookies to cool completely before removing from baking sheet. Serve.

TIP

Try crumbling cookies as a topping for lactose-free vanilla ice cream.

Calories: 90; Total Fat (g): 3; Saturated Fat (g): 1; Cholesterol (mg): 0; Sodium (mg): 70; Potassium (mg): 30; Total Carbohydrate (g): 14; Fiber (g): 1; Sugar (g): 8; Protein (g): 1. Content per serving. Assumes 12 servings.

BUCKEYE ROSES

Anyone who's lived in Columbus knows what buckeye chocolates are. I assumed just about everyone had experienced their joy while I was growing up in Ohio. However, I later discovered the privilege did not extend far beyond state lines. Here's a universally appealing buckeye rendition that eliminates butter and added sugar. Plus, its rose shape pays homage to that big bowl game in Pasadena. Serve as dessert during college football games – unless your guests are Michigan fans.

1 Place peanut butter in 12 tablespoon-sized heaps on a cookie sheet or plate lined with parchment paper. Place in freezer for 1 to 2 hours.

2 Line a mini muffin pan with squares of parchment paper. Push parchment paper into muffin holders. Paper should be crinkled around the sides.

3 Once peanut butter is frozen, place chocolate chips in a microwave-safe bowl and microwave on high for 20 to 25 seconds or until chocolate chips have melted. Remove chocolate from microwave and stir.

4 Roll each spoonful of peanut butter into a ball. Using fingers or a toothpick, dip each peanut butter ball in chocolate, leaving a small circle of peanut butter exposed at the top. Place in parchment paper-lined muffin holders.

5 Refrigerate buckeyes until chocolate is firm. Keep buckeyes covered and refrigerated for storage.

12 tbsp. creamy peanut butter, stirred and refrigerated

½ cup gluten-free, vegan semi-sweet, chocolate chips

SERVES 12
EFFORT Very easy
ACTIVE PREP 5 to 10 minutes
PAIRING Lactose-free milk or lactose-free vanilla ice cream

TIP

If peanut butter is too sticky for rolling into balls, rub confectioners sugar on fingers or outside of peanut butter to reduce sticking.

Calories: 150; Total Fat (g): 11; Saturated Fat (g): 3; Cholesterol (mg): 0; Sodium (mg): 40; Potassium (mg): 100; Total Carbohydrate (g): 11; Fiber (g): 2; Sugar (g): 7; Protein (g): 4. Content per serving. Assumes 12 servings.

HOT HONEY FRUIT

Even as a lover of ice cream and cookies, I often find a good fruit salad to be just as satisfying. When berries are in season, this honey-lime fruit dish makes a full-flavored, indulgent dessert that you don't have to feel guilty about enjoying. In fact, you'll even be working a good serving of fruit into your diet, not to mention honey and its health benefits. The cayenne pepper is what really makes this dish special, causing fruits' flavors to pop!

2 tsp. fresh-squeezed lime juice
2 tsp. honey
15 to 20 blueberries
7 to 10 blackberries
7 to 10 raspberries
4 to 5 strawberries, sliced
1 Cara Cara orange, sliced (if in season)
Confectioners sugar
Cayenne pepper

SERVES 2
EFFORT Easy enough to make after dinner on a weeknight
ACTIVE PREP 5 to 10 minutes
PAIRING Sparkling water or sparkling Moscato

1 In a small bowl, mix lime and honey together and set aside.

2 Place about ¼ cup to ½ cup fruit inside serving bowls. Drizzle with honey-lime mixture, sprinkle with confectioners sugar, add a pinch of cayenne pepper, and serve immediately.

TIP

Cara Cara oranges and pomegranate seeds work great in this recipe when in season.

Omit powdered sugar for Paleo-friendly preparation.

Calories: 90; Total Fat (g): 0; Saturated Fat (g): 0; Cholesterol (mg): 0; Sodium (mg): 0; Potassium (mg): 230; Total Carbohydrate (g): 22; Fiber (g): 4; Sugar (g): 18; Protein (g): 1. Content per serving. Assumes 2 servings.

TIP

Lactose-free frosting can be a little thin. To keep frosting atop cupcakes, I like to use a paring knife to cut a cone-shaped divot in the tops of my cupcakes. Fill the divot with frosting and lightly frost remainder of top.

VELVET DEVIL CUPCAKES

Asking me to pick my favorite dessert is almost as devilish as asking me to take only one bite if given that dessert on a platter. Nearly impossible. But if I had to choose a favorite, I'd pick red velvet cake. I love the chocolatey, sour-creamy taste and crumbly texture of the cake as much as I do the wickedly decadent cream cheese frosting. My gluten-free, lactose-free Velvet Devil Cupcakes shouldn't taste as good as traditional red velvet, but they do...and without artificial color!

1 Preheat oven to 350 degrees and line a muffin tray with cupcake liners.

2 In a medium-sized mixing bowl, combine flour, cocoa powder, xanthan gum, baking soda, and salt, whisking together until thoroughly combined. Set aside.

3 In a large bowl, beat sugar and butter at medium speed with an electric mixer until fluffy, about 5 minutes. Add eggs, one at a time, and beat. Mix in sour cream, milk or water, and vanilla. Gradually beat in flour mixture, about ⅓ at a time, on a low speed until just blended, being careful not to overbeat mixture.

4 Fill baking tray cups about ⅔-full with batter and bake for 20 to 25 minutes or until a toothpick inserted in the center of the cupcakes comes out clean. Cool cupcakes in the baking tray for 10 minutes, then transfer to a wire cooling rack and allow to cool completely before frosting.

5 To make frosting, beat frosting mix, cream cheese, and sour cream in a mixing bowl until fluffy. If ingredients are not mixing easily, add ½ tbsp. water and beat until smooth and fluffy. Refrigerate until ready to use.

6 Using a knife or rubber spatula, top cooled cupcakes with frosting and serve. Store excess cupcakes in an airtight container and refrigerate.

Calories: 250; Total Fat (g): 12; Saturated Fat (g): 5; Cholesterol (mg): 45; Sodium (mg): 140; Potassium (mg): 30; Total Carbohydrate (g): 37; Fiber (g): 1; Sugar (g): 28; Protein (g): 2. Content per serving. Assumes 12 servings.

CUPCAKES

1 cup gluten-free all-purpose flour

3 tbsp. unsweetened cocoa powder

¾ tsp. xanthan gum

¼ tsp. gluten-free baking soda

¼ tsp. salt

¾ cup granulated sugar

⅓ cup lactose-free butter, room temperature

2 eggs

⅓ cup lactose-free sour cream

4 tbsp. water, room temperature (or 3 tbsp. lactose-free milk)

1 tsp. vanilla extract

FROSTING

6 oz. gluten-free, lactose-free vanilla frosting mix, such as Pamela's brand

4 tbsp. lactose-free cream cheese

1 tbsp. lactose-free sour cream

½ tbsp. water (optional)

SERVES 12

EFFORT Reserve for special occasions, like Valentine's Day or birthdays

ACTIVE PREP 15 to 20 minutes

PAIRING Kir Royale after dinner

WATERMELON CHERRY REMIX

How refreshing! With watermelon, cherries, and a splash of vanilla-sweet-and-sour flavors, this salad serves up satisfying refreshment without restraint. This salad is best let off its leash in the summertime when watermelons and cherries are in season. Pistachios add a touch of salty creaminess, while vanilla, agave, and lime impart some sophistication – just enough to help you remember that, though this salad may refresh like Kool-Aid, it's still polished enough for a grown-up palate. Oh, yeaahh!

½ tsp. vanilla extract

½ tsp. agave syrup

½ tsp. fresh-squeezed lime juice

¼ large watermelon, chilled and sliced into bite-size pieces (about 1-inch cubes)

12 cherries, pits and stems removed, chopped

Sprinkle of pistachio meal bits and pieces

SERVES 2
EFFORT Easy enough to make after dinner on a weeknight
ACTIVE PREP 5 to 10 minutes.
PAIRING Sparkling water or Champagne

1 Whisk together vanilla, agave syrup, and lime juice.

2 Divide watermelon pieces between two serving bowls. Sprinkle with cherry and pistachio pieces. Drizzle with vanilla-lime-agave syrup. Serve.

TIP A good, ripe watermelon will have lots of "bee stings," a yellow sunspot, and will make a deep (not hollow) sound when you knock on the outside with your knuckles.

Calories: 140; Total Fat (g): 4; Saturated Fat (g): 0; Cholesterol (mg): 0; Sodium (mg): 10; Potassium (mg): 400; Total Carbohydrate (g): 27; Fiber (g): 2; Sugar (g): 19; Protein (g): 3. Content per serving. Assumes 2 servings.

TIP
....
I recommend using Brey-
ers Lactose Free Vanilla
ice cream for this recipe.

CHOCOLATE CHIP ICE CREAM SANDWICH

My neighborhood is home to an ice cream shop that serves the best ice cream sandwiches. What makes these treats are the soft cookies wrapped around the ice cream. Unfortunately, gluten and lactose sensitivities mean my husband has never tasted these delights. So I developed this recipe for extra-soft cookies - perfect for an ice cream sandwich. Don't fret if the dough turns into a giant cookie while baking! Its soft gooiness is what makes it perfect for freezing.

1 Preheat oven to 325 degrees. Line a cookie sheet with parchment paper. (Be sure to use a cookie sheet that has a lip because cookies may run).

2 Mix flax meal with water and let stand for 5 minutes.

3 In a large mixing bowl, whisk together flour, baking soda, and salt. Set aside.

4 In a separate mixing bowl, cream together butter and sugars. With an electric mixer or handheld whisk, beat in vanilla and flax meal with water until a light, creamy mixture is created. Gradually mix in flour, baking soda, and salt. Using a large spoon, stir in chocolate chips. Drop heaping spoonfuls of cookie dough onto baking sheet, leaving a few inches of space between cookies.

5 Bake cookies until edges are slightly golden, about 15 minutes. Cookies may spread to form one, giant cookie. That's okay. If you want to add a little sea salt flavor, sprinkle ground sea salt on the tops of hot cookies. Let stand at room temperature on baking sheet for 1 to 2 minutes.

6 Next, transfer parchment paper and cookies to wire cooling rack. Allow cookies to cool completely before creating sandwiches. If a giant cookie has formed, slice into individual cookies. Add ice cream between cookies to create sandwiches. Wrap in foil or plastic wrap and freeze.

Calories: 390; Total Fat (g): 17; Saturated Fat (g): 8; Cholesterol (mg): 7; Sodium (mg): 190; Potassium (mg): 0; Total Carbohydrate (g): 56; Fiber (g): 2; Sugar (g): 40; Protein (g): 4. Content per serving. Assumes 18 servings.

2 tbsp. flax meal

6 tbsp. water

2 cups gluten-free all-purpose flour

½ tsp. gluten-free baking soda

½ tsp. sea salt + extra for sprinkling

¾ cup lactose-free butter, room temperature

1 cup brown sugar

½ cup granulated sugar

½ tbsp. vanilla extract

2 cups gluten-free, lactose-free semi-sweet chocolate chips

1½-quart tub lactose-free vanilla ice cream, slightly softened

SERVES Makes about 9 ice cream sandwiches; one-half sandwich is a serving.

EFFORT Save for the weekend
ACTIVE PREP 25 to 30 minutes
PAIRING So good it doesn't need a pairing. (Aren't ice cream and cookies enough?!)

DESSERT PIZZA

Two problems occur when I eat pizza with my husband. Problem 1: We eat too much pizza to subsequently have dessert (this is my problem). Problem 2: When we don't eat too much pizza, my husband contends (convincingly) that more pizza would be better than dessert (leading ultimately to Problem 1). To resolve the issue, I invented a dish that is dessert and pizza. Cheesy, chocolaty, and decadent, we now plan ahead to save room for this preeminent pie. Problem(s) solved!

1 Preheat oven to 375 degrees.

2 Heat raspberries, granulated sugar, and lemon in a small saucepan over low heat, stirring occasionally. Heat until raspberries have formed a liquid, about 10 minutes. Remove from heat and strain raspberry juice. Set raspberry reduction aside.

3 Place chocolate chips and butter in a microwave-safe dish and heat on high in microwave until both are just melted, about 20 to 25 seconds. Stir.

4 Spread chocolate sauce on pizza crust. Lightly sprinkle chocolate with brown/palm sugar and cinnamon. Top with farmers cheese and a little marzipan or almond paste (if using).

5 Bake until cheese has melted and crust is heated through, about 7 to 10 minutes. Remove pizza from oven and top with berries. Slice into pie-shaped pieces and serve immediately with raspberry reduction to be drizzled on top.

1 gluten-free pizza crust

6 oz. raspberries, reserve several to sprinkle on top of pizza

1 tsp. granulated sugar

Juice from ¼ lemon

¼ cup gluten-free, lactose-free semi-sweet chocolate chips

½ tbsp. lactose-free butter

1 tsp. brown sugar or palm sugar

Cinnamon (optional)

2 tbsp. farmers cheese or nutmilk cheese, crumbled

Marzipan or almond paste (optional)

4 to 5 blueberries (optional)

SERVES 4 to 6
EFFORT Easy enough to make after dinner on a weeknight
ACTIVE PREP 15 to 20 minutes
PAIRING Lactose-free milk

TIP

This dish tastes best when it's fresh out of the oven. For crust, I recommend Udi's brand.

Calories: 150; Total Fat (g): 6; Saturated Fat (g): 2; Cholesterol (mg): 3; Sodium (mg): 120; Potassium (mg): 30; Total Carbohydrate (g): 21; Fiber (g): 2; Sugar (g): 10; Protein (g): 3. Content per serving. Assumes 6 servings.

(S) (VE) (VG) DARK CHOCOLATE MACADAMIA OATMEAL COOKIES

Hawaii is a magical place. Volcanoes, ocean breezes, legendary surf breaks – it's no surprise the islands are a popular vacation spot. But those aren't the only things on offer: Hawaiian foods are outstanding too. Kona coffee, coconuts, and macadamia nuts are as necessary as the beach for the complete Hawaiian experience. With these flavors in mind, I've developed a cookie that incorporates a taste of the islands and is a great complement to a cup of Kona. It's also a great post-surf snack!

1 Preheat oven to 350 degrees. Lightly grease a cookie sheet with softened butter and set aside.

2 In a large bowl, combine butter, sugar, and salt until mixed evenly. Gradually stir in oats until incorporated. Stir in egg. Fold in chocolate, nuts, and coconut (if using).

3 Place 8 to 10 spoonfuls of mixture on greased cookie sheet and bake for 10 minutes or until edges are golden brown.

4 Remove from oven and let cool for 5 minutes. Place cookies on cooling rack and allow to reach room temperature before eating. Cookies may be stored in an airtight container for up to 3 days.

2 tbsp. lactose-free butter, softened + extra for greasing baking sheet

2 tbsp. granulated or cane sugar

¼ tsp. salt

1 cup gluten-free rolled oats

1 egg, lightly beaten

¼ cup gluten-free, lactose-free dark chocolate chips

¼ cup finely chopped macadamia nuts

2 tbsp. shaved, sweetened coconut (optional)

SERVES 8 to 10
EFFORT Easy enough for a baking novice
ACTIVE PREP 15 minutes
PAIRING Kona coffee, a cup of coconut milk, or, for late-night snacking, Kahlua

TIP For vegan preparation, use vegan butter and replace egg with 1 tbsp. flax meal soaked in 3 tbsp. water for 5 minutes.

Calories: 130; Total Fat (g): 8; Saturated Fat (g): 3; Cholesterol (mg): 22; Sodium (mg): 70; Potassium (mg): 20; Total Carbohydrate (g): 13; Fiber (g): 2; Sugar (g): 7; Protein (g): 2. Content per serving. Assumes 10 servings.

TROPICAL COCONUT CUPCAKES

My Tropical Coconut Cupcakes are perfect as a fruity summer treat. Fresh pineapple gives the vanilla cake extra moisture and sweetness, while sweet coconut flakes add tropical flair. When paired with chilled white wine, these cupcakes are a wonderful finish to a meal served *al fresco*. Bake cupcakes just before guests arrive to give your home that inviting scent of warm confections. Everyone will want to skip dinner and go straight to dessert and wine. Aren't those the best parts anyway?

CUPCAKES

15 oz. gluten-free vanilla cake mix
3 eggs
½ cup pineapple juice
½ cup vegetable oil
¼ cup granulated or cane sugar
¼ cup very finely chopped fresh pineapple
1 tbsp. sweetened coconut flakes
1 tsp. vanilla extract

FROSTING

4 oz. lactose-free cream cheese
4 tbsp. lactose-free butter
2 cups sifted confectioners sugar
2 tbsp. sweetened coconut flakes

1 Preheat oven to 350 degrees. Line a cupcake pan with paper cupcake liners and set aside.

2 To make cupcake batter, combine cupcake ingredients in a large mixing bowl. Beat with electric mixer on low to medium speed until batter is smooth, about 1½ to 2 minutes.

3 Scoop batter into cupcake liners until cups are about ⅔ full. Bake for 15 to 20 minutes, until cake bounces back when light pressure is placed in center. Remove baking pan from oven and let cool for approximately 2 minutes. Move cupcakes to wire cooling rack and let them cool completely before frosting.

4 To make frosting, beat cream cheese and butter with an electric mixer on low speed until mixture is creamy, about 30 to 60 seconds. Gradually beat in confectioners sugar and coconut flakes on low speed until sugar is incorporated. Increase mixer speed to medium and beat until fluffy, about 2 minutes. Refrigerate frosting until ready to use.

5 When cupcakes are cool, spread frosting on top with a knife. Serve immediately or cover and refrigerate.

SERVES 16 to 20
EFFORT Better reserved for a weekend or special ocassion
ACTIVE PREP 20 to 25 minutes
PAIRING Bedrock Wine Co.'s Compagni Portis Vineyard Heirloom from Sonoma Valley, California

Calories: 250; Total Fat (g): 11; Saturated Fat (g): 2; Cholesterol (mg): 32; Sodium (mg): 250; Potassium (mg): 20; Total Carbohydrate (g): 38; Fiber (g): 1; Sugar (g): 30; Protein (g): 1. Content per serving. Assumes 20 servings.

TIP

I recommend using Pamela's Classic Vanilla Cake Mix for this recipe. It contains no gluten, wheat, or dairy and has a wonderful flavor and moist texture.

SEA SALT CHOCOLATE CHIP COOKIES

To my mind, there is no dessert as foundational as the chocolate chip cookie. While there may be some debate about whether crispy or chewy cookies are best, there can be no disagreement about the place of these tasty treats in providing comfort when it's needed most. Well, the comfort carries on with these cookies that are soothing, delicious, and – yes – gluten-free, lactose-free, and vegan! Let these cookies take your cares away, tender and chewy bite after tender and chewy bite.

2 tbsp. flax meal

6 tbsp. water

1⅓ cups gluten-free all-purpose flour

⅓ cup gluten-free oat flour

½ tsp. gluten-free baking soda

½ tsp. sea salt + extra for sprinkling

¾ cup brown sugar

½ cup granulated sugar

¾ cup lactose-free butter, room temperature

½ tbsp. vanilla extract

2 cups gluten-free, lactose-free semi-sweet chocolate chips

SERVES 15 to 18
EFFORT Mid-level; save for an evening with a little extra time or the weekend
ACTIVE PREP 10 to 15 minutes
PAIRING Lactose-free milk

1 Preheat oven to 325 degrees. Line a cookie sheet with parchment paper or lightly grease with canola oil or butter.

2 Mix flax meal with water and let stand for 5 minutes.

3 In a large mixing bowl, whisk together flours, baking soda, and salt. Set aside.

4 In a separate large mixing bowl, cream together sugars and butter. With an electric mixer or handheld whisk, beat in flax meal mixture and vanilla until a light, creamy mixture is created. Gradually mix in flour, baking soda, and salt. Using a large spoon, stir in chocolate chips. Drop 15 to 18 heaping spoonfuls of cookie dough onto baking sheet, leaving a few inches of space between cookies.

5 Bake cookies until edges are slightly golden, about 15 to 20 minutes. Remove cookies from oven. If you want to add a little sea salt flavor, sprinkle sea salt on the tops of hot cookies and let stand at room temperature for 1 to 2 minutes. Next, transfer cookies to wire cooling rack, allowing them to cool completely before serving.

TIP
These cookies are best served the day they're made. For vegan prep, use vegan chocolate chips and vegan butter.

Calories: 320; Total Fat (g): 15; Saturated Fat (g): 7; Cholesterol (mg): 0; Sodium (mg): 150; Potassium (mg): 10; Total Carbohydrate (g): 45; Fiber (g): 2; Sugar (g): 33; Protein (g): 3. Content per serving. Assumes 18 servings.

PUNKIN' WHOOPIES

My friend Anne makes the world's best pumpkin whoopie pies. I was lucky enough to live in the same city as Anne for two consecutive Thanksgiving holidays, and those two holidays forever made me a whoopie pie girl on Turkey Day. When we moved apart, I was almost as devastated to bid farewell to her whoopie pies as I was to her. I've taken Anne's calling card confection and "punked" it by removing gluten and lactose. Not just for Thanksgiving, these whoopies can be enjoyed any time.

WHOOPIE COOKIES

¼ cup maple syrup
8 tbsp. lactose-free butter, melted
2 eggs, lightly beaten
¾ cup canned pumpkin puree
3 tbsp. coconut flour
1 tbsp. pumpkin pie spice
1 tsp. vanilla extract
1 tsp. gluten-free baking powder
1 tsp. gluten-free baking soda
½ tsp. salt
1¾ cups cashew meal

CREAM FILLING

8 oz. lactose-free cream cheese
4 tbsp. lactose-free butter
2 tbsp. maple syrup
½ tsp. vanilla extract

1 Preheat oven to 350 degrees and line two baking sheets with parchment paper (or work in batches using one baking sheet).

2 In a large bowl, mix together maple syrup and butter until thoroughly combined. Add eggs, pumpkin puree, coconut flour, pie spice, vanilla, baking powder, baking soda, and salt to bowl and whisk together. Add cashew meal and fold in with a rubber spatula.

3 Using a spoon, drop 12 heaping mounds of batter onto each baking sheet and bake for 10 minutes or until cakes bounce back when pressed with a finger. Place cakes on cooling rack.

4 While cakes cool, combine cream cheese and butter. Whisk in maple syrup and vanilla until mixture is fluffy. Refrigerate until ready to use.

5 When cakes have cooled completely, form 12 "sandwiches," with frosting between 2 cakes. Serve immediately or store in an airtight container in refrigerator for up to 2 days.

SERVES 12
EFFORT Best reserved for special occasions
ACTIVE PREP 30 to 35 minutes
PAIRING Coffee

Calories: 300; Total Fat (g): 15; Saturated Fat (g): 5; Cholesterol (mg): 36; Sodium (mg): 440; Potassium (mg): 10; Total Carbohydrate (g): 40; Fiber (g): 1; Sugar (g): 29; Protein (g): 2. Content per serving. Assumes 12 servings.

TIP

For vegan prep, use vegan cream cheese and butter, such as Daiya Cream Cheese and Earth Balance Natural Buttery Spread.

CHOCOLATE MINT TRUFFLES

I used to count the days until Girl Scout Cookies were in season. Then, once my household switched to a gluten-free and lactose-free diet, I mourned the loss of Thin Mint cookies. Well, the mourning has officially ended – Thin Mint flavor is now always in season, fully adorned with gluten-free and lactose-free badges! My Chocolate Mint Truffles are a fantastic anytime snack or dessert for entertaining since they're small, fun to eat, and can be made in less time than it takes to snap on a green vest.

1 Line a baking sheet with parchment paper and set aside.

2 In a large bowl, combine cream cheese with cookie crumbs and peppermint or mint extract, saving some of the cookie pieces as topping. Once thoroughly combined, roll cookies and cream cheese mixture in palm of hand to make balls about 1-inch in diameter. Set aside.

3 Melt chocolate in microwave for 45 to 60 seconds, stirring halfway through. Stir a dash of extract into melted chocolate. Roll balls in melted chocolate mixture to coat. Place on baking sheet.

4 Sprinkle balls with remaining cookie pieces and refrigerate until chocolate is completely cool, about 1 hour. Store truffles in covered container in the fridge until ready to eat.

8 oz. lactose-free cream cheese, room temperature

10 oz. gluten-free, lactose-free chocolate cream cookies, finely crumbled (set aside 3 or 4 crumbled cookies as topping for truffles)

3 to 4 tsp. peppermint or mint extract + dash for chocolate

½ to ¾ cup lactose-free semi-sweet chocolate chips

SERVES Makes roughly 24 truffles – enough to serve about 12 to 18
EFFORT Very easy
ACTIVE PREP 10 to 15 minutes
PAIRING Perfect after a meal to freshen breath deliciously

TIP If the cream cheese gets too soft to roll into a ball or dip in chocolate, refrigerate for an hour to firm. For cookies, I recommend Glutino brand.

Calories: 90; Total Fat (g): 6; Saturated Fat (g): 3; Cholesterol (mg): 0; Sodium (mg): 60; Potassium (mg): 0; Total Carbohydrate (g): 7; Fiber (g): 0; Sugar (g): 5; Protein (g): 1. Content per serving. Assumes 18 servings.

SEA SALT CARAMEL CRISPY RICE TREATS

What adult doesn't love a treat that reminds them of childhood once in a while? Rice Krispie treats were a dessert I enjoyed while growing up, and my kid at heart still occasionally craves that chewy-crunchy texture. So I came up with this recipe to sate my inner child. Yes, the crispy rice and marshmallows are there, but melted dark chocolate and a dusting of sea salt prime this classic kids' treat for grown-up palates. There's no tastier way to feel like a kid again!

Non-stick cooking spray

6 cups toasted rice cereal

2½ tbsp. lactose-free butter

½ cup brown sugar

¼ cup lactose-free half and half

1 tbsp. agave syrup

1 tsp. vanilla extract

½ tsp. sea salt for mixture + extra for sprinkling

10 oz. mini marshmallows

15 wooden ice cream sticks or sturdy straws

1½ cups gluten-free, lactose-free semi-sweet chocolate chips or dark chocolate chunks

1 tbsp. canola oil

....

SERVES 15
EFFORT Very easy
ACTIVE PREP 20 to 25 minutes
PAIRING For your grown-up side, Francis Ford Coppola Winery Director's Cut Cabernet Sauvignon

1 Spray a 9-by-13-inch baking dish with non-stick cooking spray and set aside. Measure cereal and set aside in a large bowl.

2 In a medium saucepan, heat butter over medium-high heat until melted. Stir in brown sugar, half and half, agave syrup, and vanilla. Cook until mixture is thickened, about 7 to 10 minutes. Stir frequently. Turn heat to low and stir in marshmallows and ½ tsp. of sea salt. Stir until marshmallows have melted, about 1 to 3 minutes.

3 As soon as marshmallows have melted, pour marshmallow mixture over cereal and stir until cereal is thoroughly coated. Using a spatula, press cereal mixture into baking dish until evenly dispersed. Allow to cool completely.

4 Slice cereal treats into 15 cubes. Push a wooden stick or straw into bottom of each (like a popsicle). Place on baking sheet lined with wax paper to prevent sticking.

5 Place chocolate in a microwave-safe dish with oil. Heat on high for 30 seconds. Stir and continue heating until melted, about 30 to 60 seconds.

6 Dip cereal treats into chocolate as desired, sprinkle sea salt on chocolate, and return to wax paper. Place treats in refrigerator until chocolate has cooled, about 1 hour, and enjoy. Store uneaten bars in covered container in refrigerator.

Calories: 290; Total Fat (g): 10; Saturated Fat (g): 5; Cholesterol (mg): 1; Sodium (mg): 210; Potassium (mg): 10; Total Carbohydrate (g): 48; Fiber (g): 2; Sugar (g): 34; Protein (g): 2. Content per serving. Assumes 15 servings.

PB WOOFERS

If you're like me, your dog is a member of the family and, on some days, holds a higher domestic status than your spouse. Because I love my little furry friend so much, I had to include a recipe that incorporates one food he and I both love, peanut butter. This recipe uses ingredients that my veterinarian and trusted resources have said are safe for dogs (and humans) to consume. Bake these treats on a day when your pooch has been on especially good behavior. Sit. Shake. Bake!

Cooking spray

½ cup gluten-free oat flour + extra for rolling dough

⅓ cup creamy peanut butter

1 egg, beaten + 1 egg, beaten and reserved for egg wash

1 tsp. honey

1 Preheat oven to 325 degrees. Lightly spray a baking sheet with cooking spray.

2 In a large mixing bowl, combine oat flour, peanut butter, 1 egg, and honey until thoroughly combined.

3 Roll dough out to ¼-inch thickness, using extra oat flour to prevent sticking. Cut dough with cookie cutters or use fingers to shape into bones. Place cookies on baking sheet.

4 Brush egg wash over tops of treats and let stand for 10 minutes. Bake treats until golden brown, about 15 minutes. Allow treats to cool completely before serving.

SERVES 12
EFFORT Easy
ACTIVE PREP 10 minutes
PAIRING Goes great with good behavior and belly rubs

TIP

Use a toothpick to carve your dog's name (or a paw print) into treats before baking.

Calories: 60; Total Fat (g): 4; Saturated Fat (g): 1; Cholesterol (mg): 36; Sodium (mg): 30; Potassium (mg): 50; Total Carbohydrate (g): 4; Fiber (g): 1; Sugar (g): 1; Protein (g): 3. Content per serving. Assumes 12 servings.

When I'm in the mood for a mixed drink, I enjoy a variety of spirited libations. What I don't enjoy, though, is how I feel – sometimes immediately – after consuming a mixed drink with a lot of sugar or salt.

My drink recipes kick excess sugar, salt, and artificial flavor and color to the curb and stir up some naturally delicious taste.

With my Living Luxe Gluten Free philosophy in mind, I've created drink recipes that satisfy and refresh with natural ingredients and all of the luxurious flavors of classic cocktails. Indulge a little and say cheers to natural mixed drink recipes!

MARVARITAS

After a hot summer day spent wandering around in the sun, my husband and I decided it would be the perfect evening to enjoy margaritas on the balcony. With no margarita mix on hand, however, we decided to try using some limeade we had in the fridge as a base instead. Sweet (and simple) success! And our 'ritas didn't have any of the chemicals or allergens found in commercial mixes. Enjoy this drink with tortilla chips and Glorious Guacamole on a summer night for marvelous refreshment.

1 If salting glass rims, place 1 to 2 tbsp. coarse salt on a napkin. Drag a lime wedge around the rim of each margarita glass to coat with juice. Place glass rim-side down in salt and rotate 360 degrees, allowing salt to stick to rim. Fill glass with ice and affix lime to rim.

2 Pour limeade, tequila, triple sec, and lime juice into a pitcher. Stir ingredients thoroughly and serve on the rocks. Enjoy immediately!

Coarse salt (optional)
1 lime, sliced into 4 wedges
12 oz. limeade
4 oz. tequila añejo
4 oz. triple sec
2 oz. fresh-squeezed lime juice

SERVES 4
EFFORT Easy
ACTIVE PREP 5 minutes
PAIRING Tortilla chips with my Southwest Salsa recipe or my Glorious Guacamole recipe

TIP
I recommend using Simply Limeade for this recipe. Use ground Himalayan Pink Salt to salt rims and add some colorful flair.

Calories: 170; Total Fat (g): 0; Saturated Fat (g): 0; Cholesterol (mg): 0; Sodium (mg): 10; Potassium (mg): 40; Total Carbohydrate (g): 26; Fiber (g): 1; Sugar (g): 22; Protein (g): 0. Content per serving. Assumes 4 servings.

TINTO DE SANGRIA

Tinto de verano or sangria... Tinto de verano or sangria... How about the best of both? This Spanish-inspired tipple is the perfect midsummer refreshment, as much at home in glasses at the dinner table as in plastic cups around the swimming pool. Regardless of presentation, this easy-to-make drink always satisfies. Best of all, my Tinto de Sangria is a great way to use red wine if you open a bottle and decide it doesn't taste as good as hoped. Toast to an endless summer with Tinto de Sangria!

4 oz. red wine (Spanish, if available, but any red will do)

2 oz. sparkling water

2 oz. orange juice

1 tsp. agave syrup

1 thin slice of lemon

1 Mix ingredients and serve on the rocks.

SERVES 1
EFFORT Easy
ACTIVE PREP About as long as it takes to open a bottle of vino tinto
PAIRING My Patatas Bravas

TIP

This drink can be made with cheap red wine or wine that has been opened and is nearing the end of its drinkable life.

Calories: 140; Total Fat (g): 0; Saturated Fat (g): 0; Cholesterol (mg): 0; Sodium (mg): 0; Potassium (mg): 190; Total Carbohydrate (g): 15; Fiber (g): 0; Sugar (g): 7; Protein (g): 0. Content per serving. Assumes 1 serving.

THE RAZZI

When it comes to mixed drinks, I have a very girly palate. So the mixed drinks I consume have to pack enough fruity flavor to drown out the alcohol, or else I can't take a sip without wincing. This drink is great because it's easy to make, has a wince factor of zero, and is beautiful to boot. Which means that I can enjoy it whether I'm drinking it or looking at it. Of course, even for as pretty as it may be, it's still even tastier. Raise a glass to The Razzi.

5 to 6 raspberries
1 tsp. of agave syrup
1½ oz. raspberry-flavored vodka
2 oz. sparkling water
1 oz. fresh-squeezed lemon juice
1 oz. fresh-squeezed lime juice

1 Muddle raspberries with agave syrup in the bottom of a highball glass. Fill glass with ice.

2 Pour ingredients in glass, vodka first, and mix until the soda fizzes on top. Garnish with a lemon or lime wedge. Serve.

SERVES 1
EFFORT Very easy
ACTIVE PREP 5 minutes
PAIRING My Fried Calamari with Chipotle Aioli or my Truffle Popcorn

TIP I recommend Skyy Infusions flavored vodkas, which use natural flavor ingredients.

Calories: 140; Total Fat (g): 0; Saturated Fat (g): 0; Cholesterol (mg): 0; Sodium (mg): 0; Potassium (mg): 100; Total Carbohydrate (g): 13; Fiber (g): 0; Sugar (g): 8; Protein (g): 0. Content per serving. Assumes 1 serving.

BALSAMIC SPRITZER

While on vacation in the Central Coast of California, I was introduced to an unexpectedly pleasant beverage: sparkling water flavored with grapefruit white balsamic vinegar. It's one of those things you have to taste to believe how good it is. As it turns out, there are bunch of different flavors of white balsamic that can really spruce up sparkling water. Try this recipe with grapefruit-flavored balsamic first, and then branch out with any number of alternative balsamic tastes.

1 Pour several drops of balsamic into a drinking glass. Fill with sparkling water and enjoy. Add more balsamic to increase intensity of flavor as desired.

Grapefruit white balsamic vinegar
4 to 8 oz. sparkling water, chilled

TIP

Check out Trio Carmel (www. triocarmel.com) for flavored balsamic vinegars and recipes for cooking with them.

SERVES 1
EFFORT None
ACTIVE PREP Close to nothing
PAIRING My Homemade BBQ Chips and Onion Dip

Calories: 4; Total Fat (g): 0; Saturated Fat (g): 0; Cholesterol (mg): 0; Sodium (mg): 20; Potassium (mg): 0; Total Carbohydrate (g): 1; Fiber (g): 0; Sugar (g): 1; Protein (g): 0. Content per serving. Assumes 1 serving.

MOSCOW MULE

I can't exactly remember the first time I had a Moscow Mule, which I think is a testament to how much I enjoyed it (or them). Though I don't recall the specifics, I know I must have loved the drink's zesty ginger and light carbonation, rounded out by the tartness of lime and bite of vodka. That profile of flavors is still what gets my heart beating in anticipation of my first sip. To my way of thinking, there's no better beverage. Or maybe I'm just being stubborn. *Vashe zdrodovye!*

2 oz. vodka

1 oz. fresh-squeezed lime juice

1 tbsp. agave syrup

3 oz. ginger beer

1 mint sprig

1 lime slice of lime

Powdered sugar

1 In a highball glass filled with ice, stir in vodka, lime juice, and agave syrup. Pour in ginger beer and stir again.

2 Top with mint sprig, slice of lime, and a light sprinkling of powdered sugar.

TIP

For the ginger beer in this recipe, try Bruce Cost Ginger Ale, which is made from real ginger and cane sugar.

SERVES 1
EFFORT Easy
ACTIVE PREP 5 minutes
PAIRING My Marrowbones and Garlic Toast

Calories: 280; Total Fat (g): 0; Saturated Fat (g): 0; Cholesterol (mg): 0; Sodium (mg): 10; Potassium (mg): 50; Total Carbohydrate (g): 31; Fiber (g): 0; Sugar (g): 28; Protein (g): 0. Content per serving. Assumes 1 serving.

CHERRY.LEMON.MARTINI.

Shaken, not stirred, this masterful martini pairs tart lemon with a hint of sweet cherry for a killer combo of dashing and decadent flavors. Whenever I'm in the mood for a little daring and intrigue, I reach for this recipe that, though more "Bond Girl" than "007," nevertheless gives the night an undeniable edge of excitement. Whether you're planning an evening on the town or are working undercover, shake one up for a license to thrill. Martini. Cherry Lemon Martini.

1½ oz. cherry-flavored vodka

¾ oz. fresh-squeezed lemon juice + lemon peel

½ oz. triple sec

1 tsp. granulated sugar or simple syrup

Dash of grenadine

1 Fill a martini shaker with ice, pour all ingredients except lemon peel into shaker, and shake vigorously.

2 Serve immediately in a chilled martini glass and garnish with a lemon peel.

SERVES 1

EFFORT Easy enough to prepare after work or before heading out at night

ACTIVE PREP 5 minutes

PAIRING My Roasted Garlic and Flatbread or any grilled meat

TIP

I recommend using Sonoma Syrup Co. Classic Grenadine Syrup for this recipe.

Also try Skyy Infusions flavored vodkas, which use natural flavor ingredients.

Calories: 140; Total Fat (g): 0; Saturated Fat (g): 0; Cholesterol (mg): 0; Sodium (mg): 0; Potassium (mg): 30; Total Carbohydrate (g): 12; Fiber (g): 0; Sugar (g): 10; Protein (g): 0. Content per serving. Assumes 1 serving.

PRICKLY PEAR MARGARITA

When I vacation in the Arizona desert, I have a few missions that, if completed, guarantee the trip is a success: exploring the outdoors; avoiding dangerous wildlife; and, most importantly, partaking of the prickly pear margarita. Sweet, tangy, and refreshing, these margaritas are invigorating oases that turn the desert from sere to serene. The best part about my recipe is that you don't even have to brave the heat to enjoy its cool-inducing credentials. Mix one up and toast to a mission accomplished!

1 tbsp. granulated sugar + more for garnishing rims

1 lime, quartered

4 oz. tequila

4 oz. orange curaçao

4 oz. prickly pear syrup

2 oz. fresh-squeezed lime juice

2 to 4 cups crushed ice

....

SERVES 4
EFFORT Easy
ACTIVE PREP 5 to 10 minutes
PAIRING My Chorizo Queso Fundido and warm tortilla chips

1 If sugaring glass rims, place 1 to 2 tbsp. sugar on a napkin. Drag a lime wedge around the rim of each margarita glass, coating with juice. Place glass rim-side down in sugar and rotate 360 degrees, allowing sugar to stick to rim. Affix lime to rim.

2 Pour tequila, curaçao, prickly pear syrup, lime juice, and 1 tbsp. sugar into blender. Blend ingredients until just mixed, about 10 seconds. Add crushed iced to blender and blend until ice is finely ground, about 30 seconds to 1 minute. Add more ice as needed and blend to create slushy mixture. Pour into glasses and enjoy!

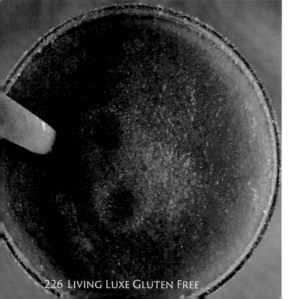

TP ....

I recommend Cheri's Desert Harvest All Natural Prickly Pear Syrup (available on Amazon.com).

Calories: 260; Total Fat (g): 0; Saturated Fat (g): 0; Cholesterol (mg): 0; Sodium (mg): 10; Potassium (mg): 50; Total Carbohydrate (g): 39; Fiber (g): 1; Sugar (g): 32; Protein (g): 0. Content per serving. Assumes 4 servings.

ELECTRIC STRAWBERRY LEMONADE

This is the perfect beverage if you'd like a little fizz to go with your buzz. Thirst-quenching, light, and delicious, this recipe was inspired by a strawberry lemonade cocktail served at a chic hotel bar in Manhattan Beach, California. I've electrified the concoction with sparkling club soda and fresh strawberries that practically pop with flavor, so it's guaranteed to charge up your night. Don't be shocked by how much you like this lively libation.

1 In a highball glass, muddle strawberries with sugar. Fill glass half-way with ice and stir. Pour in lemonade and vodka. Stir.

2 Top off with a splash of club soda (or curaçao) and garnish with a lemon wedge. Serve immediately.

3 to 4 strawberries
½ tsp. granulated sugar
3 oz. lemonade
1½ oz. citrus vodka
Club soda or curaçao
1 lemon wedge

SERVES 1
EFFORT Easy
ACTIVE PREP 5 to 10 minutes
PAIRING My Skillet Burgers and Spunky Sauce

TIP
I recommend Simply Lemonade and Skyy Infusions flavored vodkas, which use natural flavor ingredients.

Calories: 200; Total Fat (g): 0; Saturated Fat (g): 0; Cholesterol (mg): 0; Sodium (mg): 0; Potassium (mg): 80; Total Carbohydrate (g): 21; Fiber (g): 1; Sugar (g): 19; Protein (g): 0. Content per serving. Assumes 1 serving.

Included here are instructions and tips for peeling tomatoes and roasting garlic, two processes that show up several times in my recipes.

PEELED TOMATOES

This is one of my favorite tricks because it allows me to include fresh, ripe tomatoes in my recipes instead of canned tomatoes, which can leech bisphenol-A (BPA). Plus, the flavor imparted by fresh tomatoes is much cleaner and richer than any prepackaged tomato sauce.

1 Remove tomato cores, then slice an "X" shape into the skin on the bottom of each tomato.

2 Place tomatoes in boiling water until the skin begins to slacken, about 1 minute. Then place tomatoes in a cold water for 30 seconds to one minute.

3 Remove tomatoes from cold water and peel skin with fingers, starting at the "X" on the bottom of each tomato.

Fresh tomatoes

TIP

If tomatoes are left in boiling water the appropriate amount of time, the skins should come off very easily, often in a single piece.

OVEN ROASTED GARLIC

I love roasted garlic so much that I've decided to include instructions for making it here because it is the perfect spread for meats, cheeses, fruits, vegetables, and breads. Plus, it's so easy to make.

2 garlic heads, top ¼-inch of cloves chopped off with outer skin removed

1 tsp. extra virgin olive oil

1 Preheat oven to 400 degrees.

2 Place each garlic head on a separate sheet of foil and drizzle ½ tsp. olive oil on cut end of heads. Rub olive oil over the cloves to ensure it coats the tops.

3 Wrap foil entirely around garlic, place on baking sheet, and bake until cloves are soft, about 30 to 35 minutes. Cloves are ready when they can be removed from their skin with a butter knife and spread easily as a topping.

TIP ....

Be careful when removing garlic from oven, as it will be extremely hot. But don't wait too long to eat the cloves – they're at their very best when still warm.

INDEX

MANGO
Macadamia-Encrusted Mahi-Mahi 70
Samba Chicken and Plantains 117

MARROW
Marrowbones and Garlic Toast 21

MAYONNAISE
Blackened Halibut with Garlic Aioli 63
Crab Cakes 'n Football 94
Fried Calamari with Chipotle Aioli 38
Homemade BBQ Chips and Onion
Dip 28
Patatas Bravas 17
Skillet Burgers 'n Spunky Sauce 75
Spiced Salmon with Curry Dip 52
Spinachoke Dip 18
Tasty Tuna Melt 111

MILK (LACTOSE-FREE)
French Toast Casserole 167
Orange Pistachio Muffins 180
Velvet Devil Cupcakes 193
Coconut
Soy
Coconut Date Oatmeal 160

MINT
Fruit Tea Cup 172
Moscow Mule 222
Extract
Chocolate Mint Truffles 209

MUSHROOM
Crimini
Cauliflower Pasta 144
Champagne Scallop Risotto 80
Homemade Spaghetti Meat Sauce 114

NOODLE
Fusilli
Pretty, Powerful, Pasta 68
Rice
Pad Thai 99

Spaghetti
Homemade Spaghetti Meat Sauce 114
Iberian Salmon Pasta 59

OAT
Rolled
Chocolate Cashew Oatmeal Bars 178
Chocolate Chip Oatmeal Bars 174
Coconut Date Oatmeal 160
Coconut Raisin Oatmeal Cookies
Dark Chocolate Macadamia Oatmeal
Cookies 201
Granola-To-Goji 182
Peanut Butter Oatmeal 168

OLIVE
Kalamata
Sneaky Greek Salad 122

ONION
Green
Asian Fried Chicken 56
Red
Healthy Taco Salad 127
Marrowbones and Garlic Toast 21
Ms. Fit Burger 93
Shrimp on the Barbie 100
Sneaky Greek Salad 122
Yellow
Breakfast Burrito 175
Buenos Nachos 44
Caramelized Pear and Fig Pizza 55
Cauliflower Pasta 144
Champagne Scallop Risotto 80
Chicken Fajita Quesadillas 110
Chorizo Queso Fundido 14
Espinacas con Garbanzos 37
Homemade BBQ Chips and Onion
Dip 28
Homemade Spaghetti Meat Sauce 114
Homestead Quinoa Chili 108
Pierogi Mash 142
Posh Spiced Pork Chops 113
Thai Quinoa and Kale Salad 125
Salmon Curry 104
Skillet Burgers 'n Spunky Sauce 75

Southwest Salsa 35
Spanish Tortilla 66
White Chili 60

ORANGE
Hot Honey Fruit 190
Zest
Orange Pistachio Muffins 180

ORANGE CURACAO
Prickly Pear Margarita 226

ORANGE JUICE
Caramelized Pear and Fig Pizza 55
Coconut Date Oatmeal 160
Healthy Taco Salad 127
Orange Pistachio Muffins 180
Organic Berry Cherry Smoothie 165
Posh Spiced Pork Chops 113
Tinto de Sangria 218

PARSLEY
Marrowbones and Garlic Toast 21

PEANUT BUTTER
Buckeye Roses 189
PB Woofers 212
Peanut Butter Oatmeal 168

PEA
Indian Jalfrezi Chicken 85

PEAR
Caramelized Pear and Fig Pizza 55

PINEAPPLE
Tropical Coconut Cupcakes 202

PISTACHIO
Autumn Squash 145
Orange Pistachio Muffins 180
Roasted Beet Salad 131
Watermelon Cherry Remix 194

PLANTAIN
Samba Chicken and Plantains 117

Espinacas con Garbanzos 37
Spinachoke Dip 18

SQUASH
Butternut
Autumn Squash 145
Yellow
Summer Vegetable Medley 147

STOCK (GLUTEN-FREE)
Vegetable
Buenos Nachos 44
Famous BBQ Shrimp and Chorizo
Grits 87
Late-Summer Crab Grits 78

STRAWBERRY
Roasted Garlic and Flatbread 26
Hot Honey Fruit 190
Electric Strawberry Lemonade 227

TAMARIND
Concentrate
Thai Pork Curry 72
Paste
Pad Thai 99

TEA
Fruit Tea Cup 172

TEQUILA
Marvaritas 217
Prickly Pear Margarita 226

THYME
Fried Calamari with Chipotle Aioli 38
Kale Salad with Lemon Vinaigrette
129
Roasted Beet Salad 131

TOMATO
Breakfast Burrito 175
Peeled Tomatoes 231
Buenos Nachos 44
Egg and Veggie Quinoa 170
Espinacas con Garbanzos 37

Glorious Guacamole 24
Homemade Spaghetti Sauce 114
Homestead Quinoa Chili 108
Homestyle Marinara Sauce 47
Late-Summer Crab Grits 78
Ms. Fit Burger 93
Pan con Tomate 30
Pretty, Powerful, Pasta 68
Salmorejo 43
Sardine and Tomato Tosta 116
Shrimp on the Barbie 100
Sneaky Greek Salad 122
Southwest Salsa 35
Zesty Tortilla Soup 90

TORTILLA
Chip
Buenos Nachos 44
Zesty Tortilla Soup 90
Corn
Blackened Mahi-Mahi Tacos 107
Sweet Potato Enchiladas 83
Rice
Breakfast Burrito 175
Chicken Fajita Quesadillas 110
Healthy Taco Salad 127

TRIPLE SEC
Cherry.Lemon.Martini 224
Marvaritas 217

TRUFFLE
Flavored olive oil
Truffle Popcorn 48
Salt
Truffle Popcorn 48

TUNA
Canned
Tasty Tuna Melt 111

VINEGAR
Balsamic
Roasted Beet Salad 131
Watermelon and Quinoa Salad 120
Cider

Posh Spiced Pork Chops 113
White balsamic
Balsamic Spritzer 221
Buffalo Sprouts 13
No-Bones About 'Em Buffalo Tenders 33
Salt & Vinegar Kale Chips 139
White
Skillet Burgers 'n Spunky Sauce 75

VODKA
Moscow Mule 222
Cherry
Cherry.Lemon.Martini 224
Citrus
Electric Strawberry Lemonade 227
Raspberry
The Razzi 220

WALNUT
Caramelized Pear and Fig Pizza 55
Chocolate Cashew Oatmeal Bars 178
Coconut Date Oatmeal 160
Egg and Veggie Quinoa 170
Kale Salad with Lemon Vinaigrette
129
Roasted Figs with Walnuts and Honey 186
Watermelon and Quinoa Salad 120

WATERMELON
Watermelon and Quinoa Salad 120
Watermelon Cherry Remix 194

WINE
Champagne
Champagne Scallop Risotto 80
Red
Tinto de Sangria 218

ZUCCHINI
Cauliflower Pasta 144
Summer Vegetable Medley 147

GRATUITY

Many thanks to my husband for the inspiration to write this cookbook and for reading, editing, and, most importantly, tasting all of my recipes. I couldn't have completed this book without you. Thank you.

Thank you to my mom and dad for making me delicious and healthy home-cooked meals while I was growing up. You taught me the importance and joy of eating well at home.

Joanna, Nadia, Lalit, Rachel, Kevin, Anne, and Kyle, thank you for the inspiring dishes you've shared with me over the years and for your support and encouragement in writing this book.

Thank you to my mother-in-law for all the cookbooks, recipes, and cooking classes you've shared with me.

And, finally, thank you to Walter and Beth for introducing me to so many great wines, some of which are recommended here.

ABOUT THE AUTHOR

Michelle loves to cook almost as much as she loves to eat. Her culinary style reflects her passion for food as well as her time living in Madrid, Chicago, Los Angeles, Atlanta, and Luxembourg and traveling through Asia.

Having developed fantastic dishes that don't rely on gluten or lactose and that can be made and enjoyed anytime, Michelle has pioneered the art of Living Luxe Gluten Free.

Michelle, her husband, and her dog are all very well fed in Manhattan Beach, California, where they live.

Visit Michelle at www.LivingLuxeGlutenFree.com.

Eat well.

Live